Beyond HTML Goodies

by Joe Burns

Pearson Technology Group
201 West 103rd Street Indianapolis, Indiana 46290

HTML Goodies Web Site by Joe Burns

Quotes from the Media

"If you're looking for information on HTML, you'll find it here."

USA Today Hot Site

"His is a technical site that appeals to an exploding piece of the Internet pie - people building their own Web site."

PCNovice Guide to Building Web Sites

"If you are just learning, or already know HTML, this site is the only place you'll need. Expert tutorials make learning web design quick and easy. Definitely check this site out."

HTML Design Association

"Dr. Joe Burns offers help at all levels—from novice to the expert."

Signal Magazine

"Great Stuff. Probably the best overall site reviewed here."

NetUser Magazine

HTML Goodies has won over 70 awards. Here are some of the biggies:

TechTV Help Site of the Week

USA Today Hot Site

HOMEPC Magazine Best of the Web

5 Star Award - NetUse Magazine

WebMastersOnly.com Site of the Month

For a much better look at the awards (30 of them at least) see

`www.htmlgoodies.com/awards.html`

Quotes from Visitors to the Web Site

"Wow! Either I'm not as dumb as I thought or you are a very good teacher! I think it's the latter."

Greville Hulse

"This is not only a first-rate page, but is also a huge help to me, and, my guess is, many, MANY people like me. These tutorials have helped me create my own page. Once again, thank you. You're terrific."

Rose Dewitt Bukater

"You probably get dozens of thank you notes each day, but I just wanted to add my own to the lot. Since I'm a just starting out in the HTML world, I've been visiting your tutorials a lot. Just wanted you to know I've learned more from your site than from any of the books I've bought!"

Dawn C. Lindley

"Dear Mr Really Smart cool-happening dude,

I would like to thank you because I have made the transition from Frontpage '98 to HTML all because of you. I spent months trying to learn HTML before I learned of your site, and at age 14 I fully understand the ins and out's of HTML 4. My Page is in the works and I owe it all to you =)"

Taylor Ackley

"I just wanted to let you know that you are doing an amazing service to all of us weekend web masters. Thanks a million! P.S. My web page looks and feels a thousand times better since I have been following your tutorials."

Aaron Joel Chettle, Seneca College Engineering

"WOW!!!!........I was referenced by some-one to your web page this morning. I was always interested in setting up a web-page, but was afraid that it would be too difficult for me to comprehend.....So my first introduction to HTML were actually YOUR primers.....and WOW!!!!!!!........I went through ALL of them this very morning with my mouth hanging wide open..... I am still so surprised that I cannot gather any words to describe to you how I feel at this moment. Herewith I want to really THANK you.......for this !!!FANTASTIC!!! web-page that you have and this amazing tutorial. I haven't had a chance to scavenge the other pages at www.htmlgoodies.com, but I will be surfing these pages quite a lot now for sure....and actually I am going there right now at this very moment in order to check out the other tutorials and goodies...."

Ludwin L. Statie

Beyond HTML Goodies

Copyright © 2002 by Que Publishing

International Standard Book Number: 0-7897-2780-3

Library of Congress Catalog Card Number: 2002105208

Printed in the United States of America

First Printing: July 2002

05   04   03   02   4   3   2   1

Trademarks

Warning and Disclaimer

Associate Publisher
David Culverwell

Acquisitions Editor
Candy Hall

Development Editor
Victoria Elzey

Managing Editor
Tom Hayes

Project Editor
Carol Bowers

Copy Editor
Rhonda Tinch-Mize

Indexer
Kelly Castell

Proofreader
Suzanne Thomas

Technical Editor
Lindy Humphreys

Team Coordinator
Cindy Teeters

Multimedia Developer
Michael Hunter

Interior Designer
Louisa Klucznik

Cover Designer
Aren Howell

Page Layout
Ayanna Lacey

Graphics
Stephen Adams
Laura Robbins
Oliver L. Jackson, Jr.
Tammy Graham

Contents at a Glance

Contents

vii

ix

About the Author

Joe Burns, **Ph.D.**, grew up in Cleveland, Ohio, and still believes that someday the Indians will win the Series. Joe has made his living as a morning disc jockey, guitar instructor, Web designer, and finally as a university professor after receiving his Ph.D. from Bowling Green State University in Ohio. Burns ran HTML Goodies (`http://www.htmlgoodies.com`) for almost eight years before walking away at the end of 2001. The site is still posted, but Joe has moved on to concentrate his efforts on teaching and writing. He currently lives in Hammond, Louisiana, with his wife Tammy and cats Chloe and Mardi. Weekdays are spent teaching undergraduate and graduate Communications and Web design classes at Southeastern Louisiana University. Weekends are spent either in the French Quarter or on his 24-foot cabin cruiser, *Goodies*.

Dedication

I've dedicated my past three books to my wife Tammy. I sat staring at my computer screen, trying to think of another person who, in my eyes, might have had enough of an impact on my life and career as she has. A thousand names ran through my head, but only one was typed.

Many people go through life not really knowing what they are meant to do. Moreover, many go through life not really finding their true partner. My life is a daily joy because I get up wanting to start the day. I finish the day wanting to come home because joy waits there for me.

I can't even imagine what I would be doing or feeling right now had we not met. I wouldn't be doing this… I can tell you that for sure.

For everything she was, she is, and what she is certainly to become, I dedicate this fourth book to my wife Tammy.

Once was such a beautiful while that still makes me smile…

Acknowledgments

During the past two years, I've come to know two people who have helped me tremendously, but I couldn't pick them out of a crowd to save my life. I only know them through e-mail. Thanks for everything to Victoria Elzey and Brad Jones. Here's to meeting you face to face one day. Kudos also go out to Todd Green. Good luck in the new position. Sorry to see you move up. The incomparable Lindy Humphreys deserves her name in lights. Thanks to the gang at Internet.com and EarthWeb, now Dice. The good people of Southeastern deserve a round on me for being there at every turn. Thanks Karen, Steve, Joe, Win, Lynn, Jack, Mike, and all the rest. Mom and Dad get the thumbs-up for again being a two-person ad agency. They buy copies of all my books and give them to libraries. Cool, huh? I was raised by good people. Finally, thanks to my immediate family, Tammy, Chloe, and Mardi. It's amazing how quiet it can be when they know I'm working on a book.

We Want to Hear from You!

As the reader of this book, *you* are our most important critic and commentator. We value your opinion and want to know what we're doing right, what we could do better, what areas you'd like to see us publish in, and any other words of wisdom you're willing to pass our way.

As an executive editor for Que Publishing, I welcome your comments. You can email or write me directly to let me know what you did or didn't like about this book—as well as what we can do to make our books better.

Please note that I cannot help you with technical problems related to the *topic* of this book. We do have a User Services group, however, where I will forward specific technical questions related to the book.

When you write, please be sure to include this book's title and author as well as your name, email address, and phone number. I will carefully review your comments and share them with the author and editors who worked on the book.

Email: feedback@quepublishing.com

Mail: Candy Hall
            Executive Editor
            Que Publishing
            201 West 103rd Street
            Indianapolis, IN 46290 USA

For more information about this book or another Que title, visit our Web site at www.quepublishing.com. Type the ISBN (excluding hyphens) or the title of a book in the Search field to find the page you're looking for.

Introduction

If you're reading this passage, more than likely you're attempting to decide whether you should buy this. If you've already purchased the book, you're probably wondering what to do with it. Here's the scoop.

This is the fourth book in the Goodies series. If I were to give this book a label, it would end up being the "advanced" Goodies book. This book assumes that you already know something about HTML and how to build basic Web pages. I am not talking to the brand new Web designers of the world here.

The content within these pages comes from the writings I created and posted to the HTML Goodies Web site (http://www.htmlgoodies.com). To that end, this book, being forth in the series, follows the same evolution as the site. When I began writing HTML Goodies, I was rather new to the Web page game, and thus what I wrote was geared more to the beginning developer. Introductory lessons, what I termed *primers*, were posted so that anyone with a computer could get up and running.

As the HTML Goodies site went on, the primers gave way to *tutorials*. These were self-contained lessons. At first, the tutorials stayed within specific areas. There were the table tutorials. There were the frames tutorials. There were the forms tutorials. Each was devoted to a smaller sub-section of the whole. Users could come in, read up on only a section of a certain topic, and take away a new trick to try on their own sites.

Then, about four years into the life of the Web site, I had covered all the basics. The tutorials began to become advanced to the point where they weren't covering part of a topic anymore but rather an event. Instead of being as self-contained as they once were, the tutorials began to assume that the reader knew something coming in. More and more, topics were being suggested by readers. People could read my tutorials faster than I could write them, so the email began to pour in from people who had been through the primers and tutorials and now wanted to know how to do this little trick or that specific effect. The tutorials were moving away from a look at a smaller part of a larger topic and began standing on their own.

In short, each tutorial was a two-to-four page explanation of a specific event. A letter would come in from someone asking how to do a specific something, and a tutorial would go out with the answer.

This book contains all those answers.

Each tutorial inside this book is a tip or a trick that you can, hopefully, incorporate into your current Web site. Most readers will find themselves reading through the topic titles and picking out the elements they'd like to try.

My first book, *HTML Goodies*, grouped tutorials so that the book read almost like a university text. A professor could have used the book to teach a class because the tutorials were in a specific order, gradually getting more difficult and in depth as the page count went up.

This book is different in that the tutorials are all standalone pieces. Each is an entity unto itself. The works are loosely grouped into three sections, but that's basically done so that you can find the areas you're interested in more quickly.

These are the advanced tutorials. The topics within these tutorials are meant to add spice and flair to your Web pages. They are certainly not meant to be the end all. Many tutorials create events that your users will never see, but the event will help them nonetheless.

So read through the topics. Delve into a tutorial. See if it fits your page, your site. Decide whether the event will help your page, the site, or more importantly, your users.

They come first.

This book is the sum total of the last half of my time writing for the HTML Goodies Web site. I believe what is contained within will be helpful to you because most of what's contained within was requested by people just like you.

Enjoy it. I certainly enjoyed writing it.

Part I

Text and Images

Chapter 1

Neat Stuff with Text

Many people think that text is a simple and routine element of making a Web site—just slap on some font size tags, enter the text, and that's it. But there are many other cool things you can do with HTML to enhance your text. The techniques covered in this chapter are

- HTML+Time
- Perl SSI: The Include Command
- ASP SSI Example
- SSI: Dates and Time Includes
- SSI: File Returns
- JavaScript Escape Characters
- JavaScript Tabs

HTML+Time

When you own as many reference books as I do, you tend to actually sit around and wait for commands that are not yet active to become active. Yes, I know it's sad, but what are you going to do? There's nothing good on television.

You can find this tutorial, and all of its examples, online at http://www.htmlgoodies.com/ *beyond/htmltime.html.*

 You can download just the examples at http://www.htmlgoodies.com/wpg/.

I was made aware of HTML+Time a good year before I wrote this tutorial. I grabbed some code. It didn't work. I fiddled with it. No dice. I posted queries to newsgroups. Blank. It was, and still is, the only time in my HTML career that I ran into a command that promised it would work, but didn't. If all goes as planned, HTML+Time is supposed to allow you control of when elements on your Web page will display. If you want text to pop up after 10 seconds, great. If you'd like that text to split after five seconds, great. That's what this HTML+Time does, or is supposed to do.

Well, wait no more because with the advent of MSIE 5.5, Microsoft has incorporated a new element into its *Document Type Definition (DTD)*. It's called time2. As I understand it, the command time was supposed to go live when I was first looking for it, but it didn't. It was submitted to the W3C as version 1.0, but apparently (my emphasis) didn't get into the DTD for 5.0. The 2.0 version of HTML+Time is in 5.5, and the time command has been upgraded to time2 and now carries the properties I was led to believe the first time carried.

By the way, you can read all about DTDs online at http://www.htmlgoodies.com/tutors/descript.html.

I really like this effect. I dislike that it is only available on IE 5.5. If you want to use it, feel free. Netscape renders the text perfectly. It just doesn't have the delay as the seconds pass; everything displays straightaway.

Just make sure that the text you use doesn't rely heavily on the fact that it pops in after a short amount of time. That way, you can use the effect on your pages and those who cannot see the effect still get the most out of the page.

Did you get all that? There will be a test.

Make the Text Show Up

This is about as simple an example of the code as I can create. I am using the SPAN command to carry the time commands that will affect the text. If you're using MSIE 5.5, you should see a line of text. After that, you should see a new blob of text every second for five seconds. It looks something like Figure 1.1.

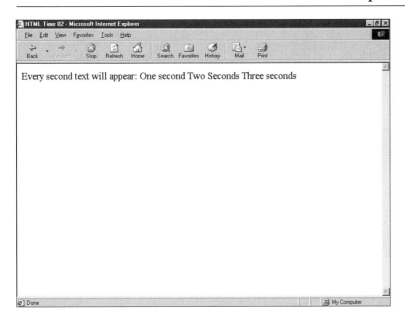

Figure 1.1
Up comes the text every second.

Did you see it? Now that's cool. I'm sure your mind is going nuts just like mine was, thinking about all the neat effects you can get with this. Let's take a look at the code. It's a heck of a lot easier than you might first think:

```
<STYLE>
 .time { behavior: url(#default#time2);}
</STYLE>
<SPAN>Every second text will appear:</SPAN>
<SPAN CLASS="time" BEGIN="1">One second</SPAN>
<SPAN CLASS="time" BEGIN="2">Two seconds</SPAN>
<SPAN CLASS="time" BEGIN="3">Three seconds</SPAN>
<SPAN CLASS="time" BEGIN="4">Four seconds</SPAN>
<SPAN CLASS="time" BEGIN="5">Five seconds</SPAN>
<SPAN CLASS="time" BEGIN="6">Done!</SPAN>
```

First, you *must* notice the Style Sheet command stuck in there. If you do not have a style block on your page, create one. You can simply write in what I have previously. It works just fine.

The time command is a class that attaches to the text in the block of code below it with the behavior you're attempting to create. See the time2 in the style command? That allows all this to finally work. Let's look at one of the lines of code:

```
<SPAN CLASS="time" BEGIN="1">One second</SPAN>
```

Here's what's happening:

- SPAN is an MSIE-only command that allows Style Sheet commands to be carried along and applied against the text without any other modification like a <P> or <BR>.
- CLASS="time" attaches the line of text to the Style Sheet statement you put in your style block.
- BEGIN="#" denotes the amount of seconds to wait before display.

If you follow down the row, you'll notice that I have each piece of text set to appear one second after the previous. That's why they come up in succession.

Appear and Go Away

With one extra attribute, you can also set the amount of time a line of text stays on the page—such as in Figure 1.2.

Figure 1.2
The previous text disappears when the new one shows up.

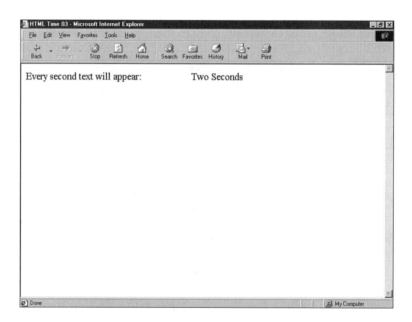

Here's the code that did it:

```
<SPAN>Every second text will appear:</SPAN>
<SPAN CLASS="time" BEGIN="1" DUR="1">One second</SPAN>
<SPAN CLASS="time" BEGIN="2" DUR="1">Two seconds</SPAN>
<SPAN CLASS="time" BEGIN="3" DUR="1">Three seconds</SPAN>
<SPAN CLASS="time" BEGIN="4" DUR="1">Four seconds</SPAN>
```

```
<SPAN CLASS="time" BEGIN="5" DUR="1">Five seconds</SPAN>
<SPAN CLASS="time" BEGIN="6">Done!</SPAN>
```

It's just the same as the previous code except I added the attribute DUR— which stands for duration. Again, whatever number you put in, that's the number of seconds the text stays on the page before disappearing. I set them all to a one-second duration to create the effect that the next text replaced the previous. As you might have guessed, if you don't use the DUR attribute, the text stays for good after it appears.

Appear in the Same Place

Some people want the text to replace the previous text instead of following it and in a different area. This example shows how to do this with text, but you can easily see how this can be used to run a slide show of images. Figures 1.3a-1.3c illustrate this effect.

 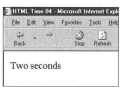 

Figures 1.3a-1.3c
Each piece of text comes and goes in the same space.

Here's the code that does it:

```
<SPAN STYLE="position:absolute;top:10;left:10" CLASS="time" BEGIN="0" DUR="1">
Every second text will appear:</SPAN>
<SPAN STYLE="position:absolute;top:10;left:10" CLASS="time" BEGIN="1" DUR="1">
One second</SPAN>
<SPAN STYLE="position:absolute;top:10;left:10" CLASS="time" BEGIN="2" DUR="1">
Two seconds</SPAN>
<SPAN STYLE="position:absolute;top:10;left:10" CLASS="time" BEGIN="3" DUR="1">
Three seconds</SPAN>
<SPAN STYLE="position:absolute;top:10;left:10" CLASS="time" BEGIN="4" DUR="1">
Four seconds</SPAN>
<SPAN STYLE="position:absolute;top:10;left:10" CLASS="time" BEGIN="5" DUR="1">
Five seconds</SPAN>
<SPAN STYLE="position:absolute;top:10;left:10" CLASS="time" BEGIN="6">
Done!</SPAN>
```

I made a couple of changes to the original "appear and disappear" script. First, I set the original text to stand for a limited duration so it gets out of the way for other text soon to come. I then set each SPAN to a specific position. Because all the positions are the same, they all appear one right on top of the other.

9

Perl SSI: The Include Command

This is a topic that has been requested over and over again by readers. *Server Side Includes (SSIs)* are Perl language-based commands, at least in this tutorial, that allow information to be gathered from the server. It works a lot like ASP. I have the ASP example coming up right after this tutorial, so read on.

Actually, I should say that ASP works a lot like this because Perl SSI was around before ASP. The concept is to use the server to gather and post information. That way, you're not dealing with browser version problems. The information being included is inserted in the page before it gets to the browser, so version differences never come into play.

This is a topic that has been requested over and over again by readers. It's a programming format called *server-side* because the element being included is done on the server's side, before it is viewed by the client, the user. Elements that reply on the browser to work are called *client-side* because something happens on the client's side, in the user's browser. Get it?

In this tutorial, *SSIs* are Perl language-based commands that allow information to be gathered from the server. It works a lot like ASP. Actually, I should say that ASP works a lot like this because SSI was around first. I have the ASP example coming up right after this tutorial, so read on.

The concept is to use the server to gather and post information. That way, you're not dealing with browser version problems. The thing that is being included is included before it gets to the browser, so versions never come into play.

Most UNIX servers are set up to run SSI. Those of you on Windows NT–based servers might have to go with ASP to get a lot of these effects, but check first before you decide you can't run these commands. You might be able to. Those of you who cannot run these commands will most likely be able to run an ASP equal. Again, an ASP example is coming up.

 You can find this tutorial, and all of its examples, online at *http://www.htmlgoodies.com/ beyond/ssi.html*.

 You can download just the examples at *http://www.htmlgoodies.com/wpg/*.

Can You Run This Perl-Based SSI?

The easiest way to check whether you can run the SSI is to post a file that tries to grab something from the server. Copy the following and paste it into a document:

```
<HTML>
<TITLE>Test File</TITLE>
<!--#config timefmt="%A" --> <!--#echo var="DATE_LOCAL" -->
</HTML>
```

Save it as an HTML file and upload it to your server. Then use your browser to view it. You should see the current day name: Monday, Tuesday, Wednesday, and so on. You get the idea. If you see the day name, you're good to go.

If not, try saving the file with the extension ".shtml." See the *s* I stuck in there? That *s* acts as a parsing command alerting the server that there's something on the page it has to play with.

Note

The *s* actually stands for *secure*. Usually when you see the *s*, you're dealing with a page or pages that are sitting within a secure setting such as a checkout. That *s* helps suggest to the system that something on this page requires a little more attention than simple display.

Many servers are configured to parse all pages; thus, you probably won't need to set the page to ".shtml," but you might.

If both attempts fail, you can try contacting your Internet service provider to see whether they can configure the server for you. But, they probably won't, or they would have already.

If it works, read on. You're in for some good commands ahead.

The `include` *Command*

When you mention SSI, this is the event most people think of:

> You have 500 files on your Web site. At the top of each of the files is a greeting that you'd like to change daily. You could either go into every page, every day, and change the greeting, or you could have a single text file that each of your 500 files include. Then you would change just that one text page and all the other pages would update. That's the concept of the `include` command.

Every page on the HTML Goodies Web site uses `include` commands, but you'd never know it by looking at the source code. When you View Source on one of the Goodies pages, there is text and coding galore before you actually get to the meat of the tutorial. I don't write any of that to the pages. I used an `include` to get the job done. Two lines of code, and all that text just magically pops in there.

The following sections show you how to do it.

The `file` *Argument*

Under the heading of the `include` command, there are two arguments. These arguments work much the same as an attribute within an HTML flag. An example would be the SIZE attribute within the FONT flag.

The format of any `include` command line looks like this:

```
<!--#command argument="value" -->
```

The command (in this case `include`) is followed by the argument (in this case `file`) and then what `file` represents.

Sharp-eyed HTML folk will notice that the format looks a lot like an HTML comment. Basically, it is. This command line does not appear on the page. What does appear is the file it represents.

> ### Note
>
> The format for these SSI command lines is not at all forgiving. You must do the coding correctly, or it simply will not work. If it doesn't work, there's no error message to help you. You're left high and dry and wondering what the heck is wrong. Try very hard to get it right the first time.

Follow these rules:

- Commands and arguments are in lowercase letters.
- The double quotes around the value are required.
- There is no space until after the command.
- That pound sign (#) is required.
- There is a space after the second double quote, before the second double hyphen.

Now, let's look at the format of the File Argument:

```
<!--#include file="included.html" -->
```

This format creates an SSI that includes the text found in the file `"included.html"`.

Why Use `"file="`*?*

You use `"file="` when the file that will be included is held within the same directory as the file that is calling for it. You can also use the file argument when the file is within a subdirectory of the directory containing the file that is calling for it. This is the one I use every time I create an SSI.

The `virtual` *Argument*

You would use the `virtual` argument if the file you are calling for is located in a position requiring an address starting at the server root. That's an academic way of saying the file isn't in the same directory as the page that's calling for it.

Maybe you'll set up a directory unto itself that contains all of your include files. This is a popular method of doing things. If so, you'll use the `virtual` argument to attach the SSI command to the files. Just make a point of giving the command the path from the server root, like so:

```
<!--#include virtual="/directory/included.html" -->
```

That forward slash before the first directory is representative of the server root. By using that leading slash, the server adds the domain name to the front of the address for you.

Tip

Use `file=` when the included file is within the same directory as, or sub-directory of, the page that wants it. Use `virtual=` when it isn't.

The Included File

I will talk about the file that will be included before wrapping this up. I like to use HTML files to `include`, but you don't have to. You can use a simple text file. I like to use HTML files because if they are hit upon by accident, they display. It might not be a good reason, but it's why I do it.

Do not think that because the file that is being included is set to the extension `.html` that it has to be a fully formed HTML document. It does not. If all you want to include is one line of text, that's all that should be on that file. If you include a title and a body command and all the other items required of a traditional HTML document, all that will be included in the SSI and you do not want that.

So...in the file you are setting up to be included, put only what you want to be included in that file, nothing more. Yes, it'll look sparse, but remember that it should not be standing on its own anyway. It is to be included in another fully formed HTML document.

I want to remind you that I have two other tutorials dealing with SSI Dates and Times and SSI File Returns. Take a look at them both. I think you'll find them useful. They follow the ASP SSI example in the next section.

Good luck with these. I hope your server allows you to play with them!

ASP SSI Example

Performed with a Twilight Zone voice…

You're surfing along and everything looks okay, but then you look up at the location bar. There's no .html up there. It's new. Instead there's an .asp sign post up ahead. You have entered the Active Server Page zone.

And there's probably a monkey tearing up the wing outside the window. Now, here's the fun part. I get to try and explain this Active Server Page process in 1,000 words or fewer. To get a better handle on all this, I actually hired a guy to sit and talk with me for a couple of hours and explain it all. It's amazing how expensive brainy people are. These are the types of things I do for you people.

The purpose of this tutorial is to get you somewhat familiar with the ASP process equal to the previous Perl SSI tutorial, and hand out an ASP SSI example for you to play with on your own pages.

 You can find this tutorial online at http://www.htmlgoodies.com/beyond/asp.html.

ASP, What's That?

ASP is actually a pretty interesting way of doing things. I will attempt to get it all into a nutshell.

If you haven't connected the dots yet, ASP are initials that stand for Active Server Pages. The concept is pretty straightforward. Imagine that you have an office with 50 people. Each of them has his own phone line. You would like to show their phone usage, a very business way of saying *bill*, over the Internet. You could do it by creating 50 different pages every night at midnight when the phone bill is compiled. That would work, but would be very labor intensive. Or you could set up an ASP system to do the work for you.

You would create a text-based page and give it an .asp extension. The page would act as a template for the 50 different pages it will produce. Employee A logs in and offers a password to prove that he is who he says he is. The ASP page is then called on. The template grabs the person's name, along with a few other basic items found in an employee database set up on the same server as the page. Then a second database, the one with all the phone records, is contacted and that person's phone usage is gathered.

All these pieces of information are then displayed to the viewer in the form of an HTML page. You can look at the source code, but you won't see the template. You'll see the HTML code produced by the template. All the work is being done by the server rather than by coders. It's all very clever.

Where ASP really shines is that it doesn't involve the browser to do the work. At the moment, there are a lot of error messages being thrown around the Web because a person is attempting to look at a Web page designed specifically for Internet Explorer using Netscape Navigator. ASP skips all that hassle.

ASP does all its magic before the browser gets the page, so what browser the user has matters very little. The server does all the work rather than relying on the browser to read all the tags.

Is ASP a Language?

ASP is not a computer language. ASP is the name of the process. The computer language most commonly used to make Active Server Pages is Microsoft's VBScript. The reason is that ASP itself comes from the utility research kitchens of Microsoft.

My ASP wizard informs me that ASP style events can be created using JavaScript, Perl, and C++, but true ASP is done using VBScript.

Can Anyone Use ASP?

ASP has to be run by a specific type of system. You might have heard that ASP was a "Microsoft" thing. It is. Your server must be running the Microsoft *Internet Information Server (IIS)* operating system, version 3.0 or higher. If not, there's no ASP for you. And before you write and ask me, as someone always does, the answer is no. There is no way to "trick" your server into understanding and running ASP if it is not configured to do so.

However...

Mitch Vassar was nice enough to tell me that you can play with ASP on your own computer running Windows 95/98 by grabbing Microsoft's Personal Web Server. In fact, you might already have it. It comes bundled with the Windows NT Option Pack 4.0 and the VB 6.0 disc. You might also want to check if it's available with your version of FrontPage.

Understand that using the Personal Web Server only enables you to play with ASP on your own computer. You cannot just upload it and get your server to run it.

Test for ASP Yourself!

Every so often, I get a letter from a Webmaster telling me to stop telling my readers to ask their Webmasters if the server is configured a certain way. It can get tedious answering the same question again and again.

So what I'm going to do is give you a very simple ASP "template" page that you can copy, paste, and post to your system. Then go look at it with your browser. If you see the correct results, you're in. Here you go:

```
<%@ LANGUAGE="VBSCRIPT" %>
<!--- You should get --->
<!--- current system date and time --->
<HTML>
<HEAD>
<TITLE>ASP Test Page</TITLE>
</HEAD>
<BODY>
Today's date and time is <%=Now()%>.
</BODY>
</HTML>
```

Copy everything and write it to a text editor. Make sure that you then save it to a file in text-only format just like you would any other HTML document.

Save the file as **test.asp**. Do not save this with an `.html` suffix. If you do, you'll kill the entire test.

Next, you'll FTP the file to your Web server. You must look at this test file from your server rather than your hard drive if you want to get a true reading. The reason is that this file uses VBScript, which Internet Explorer understands just fine. It might give you the correct results from your hard drive. That's not good.

Finally, go look at the file online. You do not have to "turn it on" like certain files in UNIX. If you have the right server operating system, it'll just work. If you get this,

> Today's date and time is

You do not have ASP abilities. If there's a date after that line, you're in!

A Useful ASP Example: SSI

After talking with my ASP wizard, I asked him if he could write a few useful ASP examples that I could hand out to people online. He said he would...for a nominal fee. I really have to look up what the word *nominal* means when I get a chance.

Dig this: You have a series of 500 pages again. At the top of every page, you want to put a greeting that you'll update everyday. You can go in and change all 50 pages, each time you change the text, by hand, but that's a killer in terms of time.

But imagine if your daily greeting is simply a page unto itself. Then, on each of the 500 pages, you had a line of code that would take what was on the greeting document and post it to the page. That way, when you update the greetings page, you update all 500 pages because they all have the same line of SSI code. And wherever that SSI code sits is replaced with the text on the greeting page when the page is loaded.

It sure would make updating pages quicker. I know. I use SSIs all the time on the HTML Goodies pages. I just use a different method than this one I'm about to give you, but that's another tutorial. In fact, it's the one previous to this one.

How You Do It

First, this is an ASP event, so you must be running this off of a server that can do it. What browser the user has is immaterial. The server is the key with ASP.

We create the page that contains the text to be inserted. I called it the "greeting" page in the preceding example. This text can be anything including HTML code or scripting. The server doesn't care. It's just going to replace the SSI command with whatever is on this page. Just remember, this page does not have to be a fully formed HTML document, or any type of document for that matter. It can be a line of text with no alterations at all. Whatever is contained will simply be included where another page has the SSI command.

Save the page with a name and an .asp extension. It has to have the .asp extension. For this example, we'll say we named the file greeting.asp.

Next we'll create the page that is calling for the text included in greeting.asp.

Each page that will contain the SSI needs to be saved with the .asp extension. Always. No exceptions.

In addition, all pages that will contain the SSI will need to have this as its first line:

```
<%@ LANGUAGE="VBSCRIPT" %>
```

Insert the previous line above everything, including the DTD and the <HTML>. Always. No exceptions.

Now here's the simple part. Wherever you want the text of the file greeting.asp to appear, place this command:

```
<!-- #INCLUDE FILE="greeting.asp" -->
```

When the page loads to the browser window, you'll have the text of the file greeting.asp where the preceding SSI command was placed. The source code will never show that command, just the text from the other file.

It's a very slick little system. Remember that the preceding SSI command is set up to display a file called greeting.asp. You'll need to change out the filename to whatever you name your own inclusion file.

So go! Find out for yourself if you can run Active Server Pages. If so, you're in for some fun. My server at school has ASP capabilities. It's really slick, and a lot of fun to play with.

SSI: Dates and Time Includes

This is the second in a series of three tutorials on SSIs. These are commands from the Perl language that allow you to include files and information right from the server.

If you haven't already, take the time to read the original SSI tutorial first.

In that tutorial, you'll get a little script that allows you to test your server to see whether you're even able to play with these commands, and a lesson on the include command. It's best that you do read it first because I'm going to assume that you have at this point and just bull forward.

 You can find this tutorial, and all of its examples, online at *http://www.htmlgoodies.com/ beyond/ssi_datesandtimes.html.*

 You can download just the examples at *http://www.htmlgoodies.com/wpg/.*

Config and Echo

Let's talk about the basic format first. After we have that, the rest is a simple chart of what argument returns what. Here's the format:

```
<!--#config timefmt="--" --> <!--#echo var="DATE_LOCAL" -->
```

The format for these includes is quite rigid. You must keep it the same. Do not put in spaces where they don't now appear. HTML is flexible. This is not. The biggest mistake I make is not having a space just before the final two dashes at the end of the command lines. Make sure that's in there. You don't get error warnings with these commands. They simply fail to work, and you can spend hours trying to figure out what's wrong when it's only a missing space.

The point I'm making is to not mess with the layout of the command line.

That being said, look at what we have here. It's actually two command lines, one after the other. The first command line denotes the time format and the second echoes it. See that?

I'll start with the second one because that one requires the least amount of work. In fact, it requires no work. Leave it the way it is. The echo command should always have the var argument set to DATE_LOCAL, in caps, with an underscore between the words.

Every time you set an include to grab a date or a time, always follow the include with this echo command line so that it echoes back and gets posted to the page.

I think I've driven that point into the ground.

The `timefmt` Argument

Moving backward, we get to the first command line. That's the one that reads `#config timefmt="--"`.

The leading pound sign (#) is required. Keep it. The argument `timefmt=` is used every time you want to return a date or time. The big question is what you want returned. There are 21 choices, each identified by a percent sign, and a one-letter code that goes in between the quotes following `timefmt=`.

The Codes

The codes make little sense to me. They don't seem to represent what they return, so you'll need some kind of chart to keep them straight. I have one in Table 1.1.

I'll use the first code, `%a`, to demonstrate a command line. The code `%a` returns the abbreviated weekday name. The command would look like this:

```
<!--#config timefmt="%a" --> <!--#echo var="DATE_LOCAL" -->
```

And here's what it gives you: `Fri`

Table 1.1 shows all 21 `timefmt` arguments and what you'll get by using them.

Table 1.1   `timefmt` **Arguments**

Argument	What You Get
%a	Abbreviated weekday name
%A	Full weekday name
%b	Abbreviated month name
%B	Full month name
%c	Preferred date and time
%d	Day of month as digit
%H	Hour number (24-hour clock)
%I	Hour number (12-hour clock)
%j	Day of the year number
%m	Month as digit
%M	Minute number
%p	a.m. or p.m.

Table 1.1   `timefmt` **Arguments continued**

Argument	What You Get
%S	Seconds number
%U	Week number/Sunday as day one
%w	Day of the week number
%x	Preferred format without time
%X	Preferred format without date
%y	Two-digit year number
%Y	Four-digit year
%Z	Time zone

You might notice that some of the elements claim they represent the "preferred" format. The word "preferred" means the default settings of the server. Default settings differ from server to server.

Notice also that these returns are from the server. If you are in one time zone and the server is in another, the time zone the server is in will be reflected in the returned values.

Multiple Codes

The codes from Table 1.1 can be used one right after another to create a longer date/time stamp. Let's say you want something that looks like this:

Wednesday, January 26, 2000

You could set up an SSI that looks like this:

```
<!--#config timefmt="%A, %B %d, %Y" --> <!--#echo var="DATE_LOCAL" -->
```

See how one just followed the other? The commas are in there, too. You can make up any combination you want by just following one with the other, leaving spaces and putting commas where you want them. It's very cool.

These are great includes. My school Webmaster uses them to death. Hopefully, you too can find a use for them.

SSI: File Returns

This is the third in a series of SSI tutorials.

 You can find this tutorial, and all of its examples, online at `http://www.htmlgoodies.com/ beyond/ssi_files.html`.

 You can download just the examples at `http://www.htmlgoodies.com/wpg/`.

The echo *Command*

Really smart readers will remember this command from the SSI Date and Times tutorial. I mean, it was just last lesson, but I like to remind you again and again, so…

In that tutorial, we used the echo command in tandem with the timefmt argument to return dates and times. Here, I want to show you four more arguments that go along with the echo command.

The first stands apart from the other three, so I'll use it to show you the format:

```
<!--#echo var="DATE_GMT" -->
```

The DATE_GMT value returns Greenwich Mean Time from the server. That basically stands alone. The next three are used to return information about the current document (the document that the command is sitting on):

```
<!--#echo var="Document_Name" -->
```

Returns the name of the document.

```
<!--#echo var="Document_URI" -->
```

Returns the path to the document plus its name.

```
<!--#echo var="Last_Modified" -->
```

Returns when the document was last posted to the server.

Just plop the commands onto the page where you want them. That's easy enough.

The flastmod *Command*

The flastmod command is created by pushing together the text, "file last modified."

This might sound much the same as the preceding echo var="Last_Modified". It is, but with one major difference: The echo command only deals with the document it is sitting on, whereas the flastmod command allows you to return data from any file. Here's the format:

```
<!--#flastmod file="page.html" -->
```

The argument is file and is pointing at the file to describe. If you want to point to a file sitting somewhere other than the current directory, put in the full path:

```
<!--#flastmod file="/dog/tree/page.html" -->
```

The only downfall I've found is trying to attach to a file on another server, which is no good. The file should be on the same server.

The `fsize` Command

`fsize` means file size. This command works the same way as the `flastmod`, allowing you to attach it to any file on the server following this format:

```
<!--#fsize file="page.html" -->
```

The command returns the size of the file you point it toward. Try it with both HTML and image files.

JavaScript Escape Characters

I get letters now and again asking how people are able to create such great looking alert and prompt boxes. Readers want to know how people get line breaks and double and single quotes to show up so nicely.

This also translates to any JavaScript commands that write to the page, including the `document.write` command. I know you've hit this wall. You write a script and you'd like to put in a single quote as in the word "you'll" or "you're." *You* know it's a single quote, but the darn JavaScript interprets it as the end of the line. Ugh! When will they build a computer that can read our minds? Is that too much to ask?

I guess it is. Until the mind-reading computers come out, using a single quote in a JavaScript line means one thing… Error!

But fear not. Learn these few simple escape characters, and you'll be well on your way to putting quotes, returns, and tabs all over the JavaScript place.

 You can find this tutorial, and all of its examples, online at `http://www.htmlgoodies.com/beyond/escapecharacter.html`.

 You can download just the examples at `http://www.htmlgoodies.com/wpg/`.

The Prompt Example

Let's do the prompt first. I made it pretty small on text. Figure 1.4 shows what happens when you click the button.

Here's the code:

```
var name = prompt("Please write your \'name\' in the box\r
Write it with \"quotes\" like this.","");
```

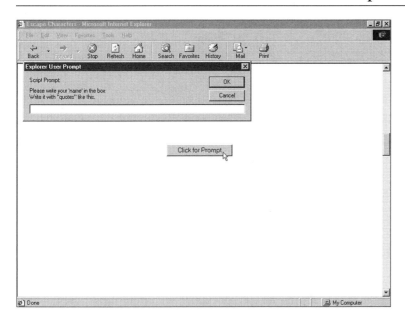

Figure 1.4
Notice the text formatting on the prompt box.

Look closely. You'll notice the following:

- The single quotes were created with \'.
- The carriage return was created with \r.
- The double quote was created with \".

The backslash is the key. If you plop that in front of the quotes or the letter *r*, you escape the coding long enough for the script to understand that you want the character to represent text rather than a command to be used in the coding. That's why we call it an escape character. Get it?

It even works in Alert commands. How about an example?

The Alert Example

I used all four characters in this example. The escape character for a tab return is the new one. It's the \t format you'll see in a minute. Note that I sometimes used two escape characters in a row to get a double tab or a double return.

The effect is shown in Figure 1.5.

Figure 1.5
Now that's a great alert box!

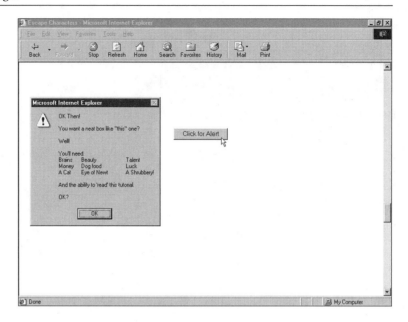

Here's the code. This should all be written on one long line. It's probably truncating on your page though. Just make a point of going through it piece by piece, and you'll see each of the escape characters at work.

```
alert('OK Then!\r\rYou want a neat box like \"this\" one?\r\rWell!\r\rYou\'ll
   need:\rBrains\tBeauty\t\tTalent\rMoney\tDog food\t\tLuck\rA Cat\tEye of Newt\t
   A Shrubbery!\r\rAnd the ability to \'read\' this tutorial.\r\rOK?')
```

Get it?

The `document.write` *Example*

You wouldn't want to use the return character in a `document.write` because it's better to literally write a `<BR>` or `<P>` flag to the page. These escape characters come in real handy when you need to use a double or single quote, yet you do not want to end the line. For example, the line in Figure 1.6 was written with a `document.write` command.

Does anybody else have parents who sounded like that? Mine did. It was the only sentence I could think of that had a single and double quote in it. Huh, I guess I have issues to work out. Here's the code:

```
<SCRIPT LANGUAGE="javascript">
document.write('We\'re going to \"need\" to know where you\'re
➥going tonight, young man!')
</SCRIPT>
```

Figure 1.6
Aw, mom…

Note

See that little arrow icon in the preceding code? That is what we call a *code continuation icon*. Because books are written with distinct margins, we can't always print an entire line of code on one line in the book. Whenever you see that code continuation icon, it means that line needs to be continued at the end of the previous line.

JavaScript is pretty pesky about line breaks, so be sure to pay attention to those especially in JavaScript code.

Read slowly and pick out the escape characters.

I'll bet those little blips of information just made someone's life a little easier. At least now we'll have fewer alert boxes that do not talk in contractions. It is a good thing you will like.

JavaScript Tabs

The information in this tabs tutorial is contained in the preceding escape character tutorial. Because tabs always seem to be the subject of a question that comes up by itself, I decided to create a quick tutorial devoted just to tabs.

You can find this tutorial, and all of its examples, online at `http://www.htmlgoodies.com/tutors/tabs.html`.

 You can download just the examples at `http://www.htmlgoodies.com/wpg/`.

If you have as many reference books as I do, you need to stop buying them. I think I'm single-handedly keeping the computer book market up and running.

Furthermore, if you have as many reference books as I do, you have no doubt looked for a way to work with tabs in HTML. You haven't had any luck, right? There isn't even a line under "tabs" in the indexes.

I guess the main reason is that HTML is text-based, so a "tab" isn't carried along with the text much like extra spaces and carriage returns are ignored. You can produce 100 carriage returns in the HTML code, and none of them show up when the browser displays the code. Drat!

In my research, I received some letters that people were creating table formats to act as tabs. It's a good idea and it works, but it's also pretty labor intensive. Others told me they created a tabbed layout, copied and pasted it into their HTML document, and then surrounded it with the <PRE> or <XMP> flags. Sometimes it worked, but sometimes it didn't.

In order to work with tabs, you'll need a command that will "force" text to a certain point. Without that, tabs are pretty much worthless and look pretty bad when displayed. Well, after reading more than I should have, I came up with a method of writing with tabs. It involves JavaScript and the tab Escape Sequence. Don't let the name catch you off guard. It's a greater title than what I'll actually show you.

A Tab Example and Code

Figure 1.7 is a series of words set to tabs.

Here's the code that did it. See if you can pick out the tabs.

```
<SCRIPT LANGUAGE='Javascript'>
document.write("<XMP>")
document.write("100 Meter\t400 Meter\t1500 Meter\r")
document.write("110 Hurdles\tHigh Jump\tLong Jump\r")
document.write("Javelin\t\tPole Vault\tShot Put\r")
document.write("Discus")
document.write("</XMP>")
</SCRIPT>
```

By the way...do you know what the preceding list represents?

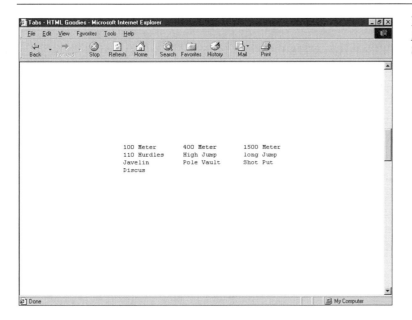

Figure 1.7
*Hmmm…let's see.
Uhhhh…what is that?*

Explanation

Looking at the code as opposed to the list, you can see the text that appeared on the page, but did you see the tab and the carriage return? Look again. The tab is represented by \t, and the return is represented by \r.

See it now?

Those two items, \t and \r, are escape characters. Remember them from the previous example? The other text is methods that would otherwise be difficult inside a JavaScript environment. Notice that there are no spaces. None are needed. Just plop in the backslash and you get the tab or the return.

I used the carriage return escape characters in this example simply to make a point. If I were writing this to one of my own pages, I probably wouldn't use the escape character but rather opt for a <BR> flag. I just think it's better coding.

You might notice that in the fourth document.write statement, there are two tab commands. The reason is, just like normal tabs, the first word was shorter than those preceding, so I needed an extra tab to force the second bit of text over to the tab setting created by the longer words in the preceding lines.

<XMP>?

I know I said earlier in the tutorial that using the <PRE> or <XMP> flag didn't work because the tabs often didn't transfer correctly—especially if you're using a non-block font. However, this is different. In this case, we do have the ability to force tabs. In just surrounding text with <PRE> or <XMP>, we do not.

If you ran this script without the <XMP> tag, the tabs would not appear. All the text would run together. You would get angry and call my mother a bad name. You would then look at your source code and see that the code is perfectly tabbed out. Remember that extra spaces and carriage returns in the code do not transfer to the display. That's why all the text runs together. By sticking in the <PRE> or <XMP> tags, you transfer the spaces to the display. In this case, it works because the text in the code is forced to tab. Simply copying and pasting tabbed text will not transfer the forced tabs. Get it?

Just like all other JavaScript I've given you, using this one is a simple matter of copying at least one of the `document.write` statements, pasting it again and again, and changing out the text you want.

After you get all the text in there, you'll probably see the need for a second tab to force text to line up. Just go back in and add another \t. Remember also that the text will not jump to the next line unless you make a point of adding a \r, or <BR> flag, to force it to do so.

Go nuts, you tab fans. This is a solid way to create tabbed tables without going to all the extra coding of actually setting up a table.

Oh, and in case you're wondering, that tabbed text shown previously represents the 10 events in the Olympic Decathlon. I plan to compete in 2000 and something. You know, whenever the next Olympics are. I'm ready.

Chapter 2

Neat Stuff with Images

There are a multitude of cool tricks and techniques that you can do with images alone that can enhance your Web site design. As with every element of a Web page, be sure to use caution and common sense when deciding what to add. The cool image techniques covered in this chapter are

- Image Slideshow Script
- Image Map Image Flip
- Dual Image Flip
- Mouse Trail Effect

Image Slideshow Script

I get a lot of email asking how people are setting up multiple image slideshows on their pages. I've seen a lot of these being used on CNN and other new pages. I'm glad for it, too. I think the programming is good design.

The basic concept is that instead of having 10 different images all on one page, you set up a JavaScript that only displays one image. The user then sees the remainder of the images by clicking on buttons or text. It's a slideshow.

 You can find this tutorial, and all of its examples, online at http://www.htmlgoodies.com/ beyond/slideshow.html.

 You can download just the examples at http://www.htmlgoodies.com/wpg/.

The Effect

I've actually had the code to do a basic slideshow in my JavaScript Primers for a while. The problem is that the CNN slideshows, the shows everyone wants, do a whole lot more than mine did. Mine simply showed the next image and then recycled. The CNN slideshows did a lot more, including going backward through the images and posting text.

So, I sat down one Saturday morning, recoded the basic slideshow, and came up with this. Take a look at Figure 2.1.

Figure 2.1
Click either way. The images and text just keep coming.

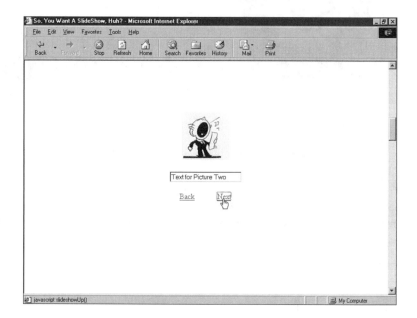

Right now it's only moving through four images. Of course, you can set it to show as many or as few as you'd like. Let's get to the code and how it works.

The Code

Here's the entire script:

```
<SCRIPT LANGUAGE="JavaScript">
var num=1
img1 = new Image ()
img1.src = "information.gif"
img2 = new Image ()
img2.src = "interference.gif"
img3 = new Image ()
img3.src = "message.gif"
```

```
img4 = new Image ()
img4.src = "nervous.gif"
text1 = "Text for Picture One"
text2 = "Text for Picture Two"
text3 = "Text for Picture Three"
text4 = "Text for Picture Four"
function slideshowUp()
{
num=num+1
if (num==5)
{num=1}
document.mypic.src=eval("img"+num+".src")
document.joe.burns.value=eval("text"+num)
}
function slideshowBack()
{
num=num-1
if (num==0)
{num=4}
document.mypic.src=eval("img"+num+".src")
document.joe.burns.value=eval("text"+num)
}
</SCRIPT>
<!-- The Image and Form Codes are Below -->
<CENTER>
<IMG SRC="information.gif" NAME="mypic" BORDER=0 HEIGHT="100" WIDTH="100">
<p>
<FORM NAME="joe">
<INPUT TYPE="text" WIDTH="100" NAME="burns" VALUE="Text For Picture One">
</FORM>
<A HREF="JavaScript:slideshowBack()"> Back</A>
<A HREF="JavaScript:slideshowUp()"> Next</A>
```

We'll start down in the image form section of the code. This is the code that makes up the stuff that actually displays on the page.

```
<IMG SRC="information.gif" NAME="mypic" BORDER=0 HEIGHT="100" WIDTH="100">
<FORM NAME="joe">
<INPUT TYPE="text" WIDTH="100"
NAME="burns" VALUE="Text For Picture One">
</FORM>
<A HREF="JavaScript:slideshowBack()"> Back</A>
<A HREF="JavaScript:slideshowUp()"> Next</A>
```

OK, it's all fairly basic stuff. We begin with an image command set to a specific height and width. The SRC is the SRC of the first image you want to display. After that, the JavaScript takes over and posts the images for you. The IMG flag is also given a name, "mypic". This becomes important further into the code.

The next element is the text box that holds the information about the image. It's a basic form element. Notice that the form itself is named "joe" and the text box is named "burns". Again, that all becomes quite important further into the code.

Finally, we have two sets of text set up to trigger two JavaScript functions, slideshowBack() and slideshowUp().

Now we'll look at the script itself...

At the top of the script is the obligatory <SCRIPT LANGUAGE="JavaScript"> statement. Then, we offer the script some stuff to play with:

```
var num=1
img1 = new Image ()
img1.src = "information.gif"
img2 = new Image ()
img2.src = "interference.gif"
img3 = new Image ()
img3.src = "message.gif"
img4 = new Image ()
img4.src = "nervous.gif"
text1 = "Text for Picture One"
text2 = "Text for Picture Two"
text3 = "Text for Picture Three"
text4 = "Text for Picture Four"
```

We start with setting a variable, num to one. You can pretty much figure out the rest on your own. The four images listed follow a traditional JavaScript format.

If it's new to you, basically we are stating a variable for a new image and then giving a source, or what you might call a location, for the new image. We're telling the script where to find it.

After that, the four blips of text accompanying each image are listed. Each is assigned to a variable name.

If you decide to alter the code and add more images, that's fine. Just be sure to continue following that same format again and again. Each new image must increase the numbers by one as those before it have done.

Now here comes the fun stuff:

```
function slideshowUp()
{
num=num+1
if (num==5)
{num=1}
document.mypic.src=eval("img"+num+".src")
document.joe.burns.value=eval("text"+num)
}
```

The first function is `slideshowUp()`. It posts the next picture in line. Remember that variable, `num`, we set previously? Well, now we play with it. The lines basically state that `num` (which started as `1`, remember) gets `1` added to it. We then check to see if `num` equals `5`. Why? Well, because there is no `5`. We're only dealing with four images here. If `num` is `5`, we reset it to `1`. That's how the function is able to loop around again and again.

Remember that, if you decide to add more images to this script. You must always set that number to one more than the number of images you have.

Now that we know which number image we're dealing with here (it's the number image denoted by what the number `num` represents), we can post the image and the text that goes along with it.

The first line sets the image name that goes into `document.mypic`. The `eval` helps to turn the text in the parentheses into a variable name rather than just text.

The next line sets the text that is to display in the text box. See how it's pointed right at `document.joe.burns.value`?

Each time you click to activate `slideshowUp()`, `1` is added to the value of `num` and the new image and text are posted.

Now we need to go backward:

```
function slideshowBack()
{
num=num-1
if (num==0)
{num=4}
document.mypic.src=eval("img"+num+".src")
document.joe.burns.value=eval("text"+num)
}
```

This is the same as the preceding function except that it's named `slideshowBack()`. In addition, instead of adding 1 to `num`, it takes 1 away. That's why it goes backward. There's one more thing: We no longer test to see whether the count gets to 5. Because we're going backward, we're interested in whether the count gets to 0. If it is 5, we reset `num` to 4. That's how it can loop over again and again. Everything else is the same.

It's actually a fairly simple script. If you add or take away images, make sure you change out the number that the functions are looking for.

Also, if you simply want the images to scroll through without any text or text box, lose the text box in the code. Then go up into the functions (both functions remember) and remove the line.

You can also delete the text:

```
document.joe.burns.value=eval("text"+num)
```

But it won't matter. It's never going to be called for, so it's not required.

Image Map Image Flip

This is a great effect. Let me tell you what it does first, and then you can try it out for yourself. Figure 2.2 is of an 1864 painting by Francis B. Carpenter entitled *The First Reading of the Emancipation Proclamation Before the Cabinet*. I've always liked it, and it lends itself to this tutorial. The picture is an image map. But wait...there's more.

 You can find this tutorial, and all of its examples, online at `http://www.htmlgoodies.com/tutors/imagemapmouse.html.`

 You can download just the examples at `http://www.htmlgoodies.com/wpg/.`

When you place your pointer over Lincoln's face, you immediately get an enlarged version of the left side of the image. Ditto the guy with the beard, a member of the cabinet, sitting to Lincoln's left. The map just flips for you. After the image is flipped, let your pointer sit for a minute. A ToolTip pops up. Figures 2.2–2.4 show the entire effect.

OK! Now that's pretty smooth. I've only set the map to do two flips in order to keep the text small enough so that you can understand it quickly, but I think you can already see the benefits of this. I could have set a flip for each of the faces. A new image could have come up telling who the person was and a little background about him. The entire scene could have been explained just by moving the mouse around. Cool!

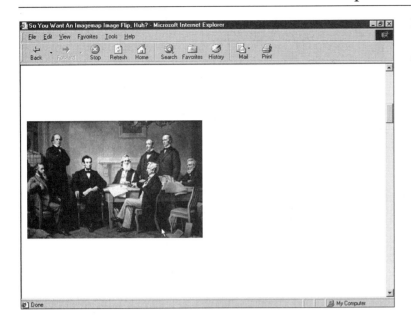

Figure 2.2
The image map before any flipping.

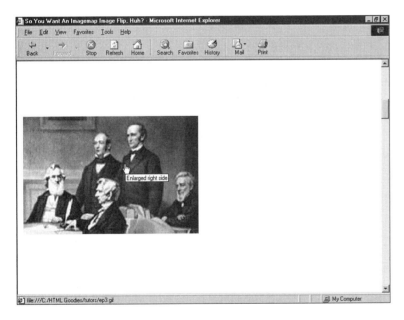

Figure 2.3
The right side showing ToolTip.

Figure 2.4
*The enlarged left side
showing ToolTip.*

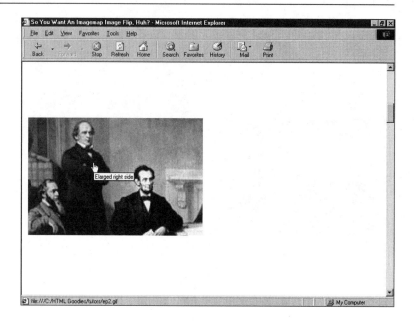

No Flipping Sections!

Some of you might have rolled into this tutorial thinking I was going to show how to flip
only one section of the image map. For instance, you roll over Lincoln's head and it
becomes Garfield (the president, not the cat). This effect can be achieved by building a
Fake Map out of image flips. Then, just that one section flips, and Lincoln becomes
Garfield. This tutorial flips the entire image.

Preload the Images

Because we're dealing with images that need to come up in a heartbeat, it's best to preload
all the ones you'll need. I did that through a JavaScript that looks like this:

```
<SCRIPT LANGUAGE="javascript">
Image1 = new Image(265,406)
Image1.src = "ep.gif"
Image2 = new Image(265,406)
Image2.src = "ep2.gif"
Image3 = new Image(265,406)
Image3.src = "ep3.gif"
</SCRIPT>
```

If you increase the number of images, you'll need to continue the same format as previously shown but increasing the numbers by one for each new image.

The Images

I want to point out something. Don't think I'm doing some wonderful trick that makes the browser enlarge the section of the image. This is a basic image flip created using three images that I put together. Each image is 409X265. I made the images that "blow up" a section of the greater image using a graphics editor. In fact, here are the three images used in the effect: ep.gif, ep2.gif, and ep3.gif.

As with most image flips, all three images are the same size on purpose.

Main Image

The code that places the main image on the page also links the image space to both the image map coordinates and the JavaScript functions that make the flip. That code is shown here, followed by an explanation of each piece:

```
<IMG NAME="emp" SRC="ep.gif" USEMAP="#ep">
```

- ● NAME="emp" names the space the image sits in. This is used in the JavaScript functions to link this space to hierarchy statements so that when an image is used to replace the space, the JavaScript knows where to put it.
- ● SRC="ep.gif" is the source for the image.
- ● USEMAP="#ep" tells the browser that this is an image map and that it can find the coordinates further in the code in a map called ep. If this is new to you, maybe a quick read of the Client Side Image Map tutorial is in order. You'll find it online at http://www.htmlgoodies.com/tutors/cs_imap.html.

The Function

Three images are involved here. Thus, you need three functions. The original image is posted by the HTML code itself. The first function flips to the second image, the second function flips to the third image, and the third function flips back to the original. It all looks like this:

```
<SCRIPT LANGUAGE="javascript">
function zoomin() {
document.emp.src = Image3.src; return true;
}
function zoomout() {
document.emp.src = Image2.src; return true;
}
```

```
function original() {
document.emp.src = Image1.src; return true;
}
</SCRIPT>
```

As I just said, there are three functions. They are named zoomin(), zoomout(), and original().

The meat of the script, the part that does the trick, is between the curly brackets. The hierarchy statement breaks down like this:

- document denotes that this effect occurs somewhere on this document.
- emp is the name of the image space from earlier. This is where the image displays—the space occupied by the original image.
- src is the source.
- Image3.src comes from the preload statements and represents the third image.
- return true allows the image to remain flipped as long as the pointer sits tight.

The order in which the functions appear really doesn't make any difference except for the original(). That one must be linked to the original image. Past that, it's much easier to alter the onMouseOver statements in the map to change what image appears than to redo all the function statements. So just make sure that you have a function named for each of the images you preloaded. As long as each function is a different name, you're okay.

The Map

It looks like this:

```
<MAP NAME="ep">
<AREA SHAPE="rect" ALT="Enlarged right side" COORDS="117,70,160,119"
HREF="ep2.gif" onMouseOver="zoomout()" onMouseOut="original()">
<AREA SHAPE="rect" ALT="Enlarged right side" COORDS="212,68,250,120"
HREF="ep3.gif" onMouseOver="zoomin()" onMouseOut="original()">
<AREA SHAPE="default" nohref>
</MAP>
```

There are three sections to this map. The first is the active site of Lincoln's head, the next is the active site over the bearded man's head, and the third is any other part of the map. Note the three preceding lines of code for each. Again, if this is new, maybe a trip to the Client Side Image Map tutorial is in order.

I am most interested in the onMouseOver and onMouseOut commands. See how the preceding two lines of code, which denote coordinates, have them? The onMouseOver should be pointing at the function that displays the correct new image. The onMouseOut should always be pointed at the function that displays the original image.

Like I said previously, it's easier to change the function names around here than to rewrite all the functions themselves.

The ToolTip Box

If you haven't caught it by now, the yellow ToolTip box is created by the "ALT=" attribute in the AREA flag.

You can set up as many image flips as you can set aside parts of the image. Just make sure that each section has its own function assigned to it. I think this is a great effect.

Dual Image Flip

I can usually tell where my readers are surfing. The reason is because often I'll get a letter asking how another site did something spectacular. The latest thing everyone wants is a dual image flip like the one put up on Comedy Central. It isn't there anymore, so don't bother looking. They had it set up so that when your cursor moved over a link on the left of the page, the image in the television screen changed. It was a great example of page construction.

 You can find this tutorial, and all of its examples, online at http://www.htmlgoodies.com/ beyond/dualflip.html.

 You can download just the examples at http://www.htmlgoodies.com/wpg/.

Here is just the effect you're looking for. By rolling your pointer over the two buttons on the left, it flips and the image on the right flips. Figures 2.5a and 2.5b show the effect.

Now that is cool! I'll state right here that you do not have to have all the images right up close to each other like I do here. That's only for demonstration's sake. They can be on opposite ends of the Web page: It doesn't matter.

The Parts

Okay, there's no doubt about it, this is a rough JavaScript. It's involved, and if you intend to alter it in any way, you're going to have to be very careful.

Figure 2.5a
Flip...

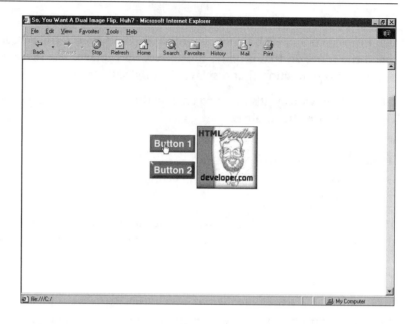

Figure 2.5b
...and flip again.

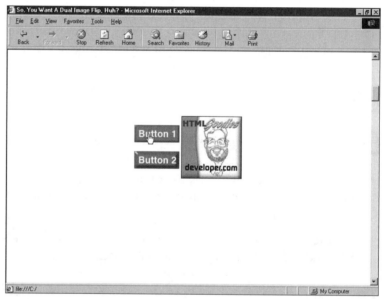

Because it's always easier to simply copy and paste from me, I've put together an HTML page you can download that contains just the working script and nothing else. It might be easiest to use this to follow along.

 All the parts you'll need are in a big Zip file ready to be downloaded. You'll find it at
http://www.htmlgoodies.com/beyond/dualflip.zip.

The Script

This event comes in two parts: the script that sits in between the page's <HEAD> commands, and the code that goes in the body commands to display the images. We'll work with the script first. I have tried to add comment statements in the following script to help you see the parts and what they do. They are also bold to help you pick them out. The comment commands are there to tell you what is happening at each stage of the script. They should not affect the script's functions:

```
<SCRIPT LANGUAGE="JavaScript">
//Below is the code that pre-loads the graphics
{
//These are the large images
alt0 = new Image();
alt0.src = "white.gif";
alt1 = new Image();
alt1.src = "hg_banner.gif";
alt2 = new Image();
alt2.src = "jg_banner.gif";
//These are the first button graphics
graphic1= new Image();
graphic1.src = "but1.gif";
graphic1on = new Image();
graphic1on.src = "but1b.gif";
//These are the second button graphics
graphic2= new Image();
graphic2.src = "but2.gif";
graphic2on = new Image();
graphic2on.src = "but2b.gif";
//This is the function that calls for
//the change in the buttons
}
function imageChange(imageID,imageName,imageID2,imageName2) {
{
document.images[imageID].src = eval(imageName + ".src");
document.images[imageID2].src = eval(imageName2 + ".src");
}
```

```
  }
</SCRIPT>
```

The Large Images

Let's take it in order, shall we? Here's the code that appears first. It denotes the large images:

```
alt0 = new Image();
alt0.src = "white.gif";
alt1 = new Image();
alt1.src = "hg_banner.gif";
alt2 = new Image();
alt2.src = "jg_banner.gif";
```

Note the format. The alt# = new Image(); statement denotes a new image and names it. The alt#.src = "--", which immediately follows, denotes the source of the image.

The order is as follows:

1. The image that appears on the page when nothing is happening
2. The image that appears when the first button is passed over
3. The image that appears when the second button is passed over

If you add images and buttons, just continue to follow the pattern, adding right under where the preceding statement left off.

The Buttons

Here's the code for the first button shown earlier. The second also follows this pattern, so there's only the need to show this one.

```
graphic1= new Image();
graphic1.src = "but1.gif";
graphic1on = new Image();
graphic1on.src = "but1b.gif";
```

The pattern should look a little more normal by now. The new image statement is used to pre-load the image; then the statement immediately following offers the source for the image. Two images are required to make the image flip, thus two images are called for. Do you see that previously? One is named but1.gif, and the other is named but1b.gif.

Again, the other image flip button follows the same format. If you do add any buttons to this, be sure to continue the same pattern, continuing where the second button left off.

The Function

By function, I mean this:

```
function imageChange(imageID,imageName,imageID2,imageName2) {
{
document.images[imageID].src = eval(imageName + ".src");
document.images[imageID2].src = eval(imageName2 + ".src");
}
}
```

Simply put, don't touch it. It doesn't need updating. It simply acts as a go-between for the code and the images denoted above it.

The Code

You're going to need the code for the images, too. This should be placed in the <BODY> section of your page right where you want the images to appear.

Please Note: I have the images inside a table format in order to get that nice block form you saw before. If you don't want that, just cut away the table commands after you get it. Here is the code for the images:

```
<TABLE border="0">
<TR>
<TD>
<A HREF="http://www.htmlgoodies.com"
onMouseOver="imageChange('global','alt1','one','graphic1on')"
onMouseOut="imageChange('global','alt0','one','graphic1')">
<IMG SRC="but1.gif" BORDER="0" NAME="one"></A>

<BR><BR>
<A HREF="http://www.javagoodies.com"
onMouseOver="imageChange('global','alt2','two','graphic2on')"
onMouseOut="imageChange('global','alt0','two','graphic2')">
<IMG SRC="but2.gif" BORDER="0" NAME="two"></A>
</TD>
<TD>
<IMG SRC="white.gif" WIDTH="130" HEIGHT="130" NAME="global">

</TD>
</TR>
</TABLE>
```

We'll start by looking at one of the image flip buttons. They are both the same, so there's no need to show both. This is the first one shown previously:

```
<A HREF="http://www.htmlgoodies.com"
onMouseOver="imageChange('global','alt1','one','graphic1on')"
onMouseOut="imageChange('global','alt0','one','graphic1')">
<IMG SRC="but1.gif" BORDER="0" NAME="one"></A>
```

Let's break it down to each line. Line one:

```
<A HREF="http://www.htmlgoodies.com"
```

No surprises here—it's the beginning of a basic hypertext link. Here's where you put in the URL of the page you want this to code to link with.

Line two:

```
onMouseOver="imageChange('global','alt1','one','graphic1on')"
```

Here's where it all happens. This onMouseOver Event Handler is calling on the function up in the JavaScript. See the name "imageChange" up in the script? Inside the parentheses is the number of items that are to be affected. There are four: the big image (global), the new big image (alt0), the image identifier (one), and the new onMouseOver image (graphic1on).

Remember that all these names were called for in the top portion of the script. Look again, and you'll see these names.

Line three:

```
onMouseOut="imageChange('global','alt0','one','graphic1')">
```

This is what happens when the mouse pulls off of the image. Notice the four items to be changed are now the images that were originally there to begin with. Thus, when the mouse moves off, everything goes back to normal. Get it?

Line four:

```
<IMG SRC="but1.gif" BORDER="0" NAME="one">
```

Here's a basic image command set up to be an active image that people can click on. Notice the BORDER="0" command to lose the blue border.

The only real new item is the NAME="one" image identifier that's used to link this image with the onMouseOver and onMouseOut Event Handlers.

</A> ends the whole thing.

Now, without going back over the entire second image link listed previously, take a look for yourself and see that all the parts are the same except that all the image names have been updated so that this button is made up of new images.

Also notice that the NAME="--" image identifier has been upgraded to "two". If you add images to this, you'll need to follow this format again and again, as well as continue to add 1 to the name and to the onMouseOver and onMouseOut Event Handlers so each new link is one up from the last. And remember, if you upgrade it in the IMG command, you also must update it in the Event Handlers.

I told you this was a little rough.

The Large Image

The code looks like this:

```
<IMG SRC="white.gif" WIDTH="130" HEIGHT="130" NAME="global">
```

This one's not so tough. It's a simple IMG command, but notice inside there's that wonderful NAME="global" command. Remember that from each of the onMouse(Over and Out) Event Handlers earlier? That's what attaches this image to those other images. It's also what denotes to the browser that here's where the new global image (denoted by alt#) is to be placed.

Okay, you have all the parts. You can look at each image, and then look through the JavaScript and see where it goes. You can then try to change out the images I gave you with new images. Then you can try to add a few new image flips that affect the larger global image.

Keep playing with it. You'll get it to work and really impress your friends. Then they'll write to me asking how you got that effect.

Mouse Trail Effect

After something new comes out, I get letters like crazy asking how to get the effect. This is just such an effect. It's been out for a while, so it's not really new, but I've held off as long as I could. Figure 2.6 is a mouse trail.

 You can find this tutorial, and all of its examples, online at *http://www.htmlgoodies.com/beyond/mousetrail.html.*

 You can download just the examples at *http://www.htmlgoodies.com/wpg/.*

You've probably seen the effect. You log in to a page and letters or images follow your pointer all over the page. Some people love the effect and others hate it. I don't mind it so much as long as the pointer element adds to the page and doesn't overtake the content. When I have to constantly move the mouse to see the text, that's a problem. Basically, if it's done correctly and in a fairly subtle fashion, it might add to the page.

Figure 2.6
Nice tail you got there, pal.

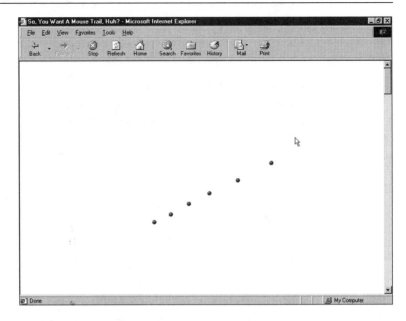

There are numerous methods of getting the effect. The problem comes in when you attempt to get the effect to work properly across browsers. Internet Explorer follows the mouse one way, and Netscape Navigator follows the mouse another.

IE First

The effect is achieved on Internet Explorer by creating a script that sees the location of the mouse as an X and Y point on the screen. A name is given to an image, and that image is told to basically put itself where X and Y intersect. Figure 2.7 shows the effect.

The script runs every time the mouse moves, and the effect is an image following the pointer. Of course, you can get the same effect with text if you set the text to a division and give the division the name. A short script by Chase Cathcart gets the job done.

The script then looks like this:

```
<style>
#pic1{position:absolute; }
</style>
<script>
//Copyright 2001 Chase Cathcart. Please leave this in here.
function trackit(){
document.all.pic1.style.left = event.x
document.all.pic1.style.top = event.y
if(event.x < "200"){
```

```
document.all.pic1.style.left = "200"
}
}
document.onmousemove = trackit
</script>
<img src="kittenrunning.gif" id="pic1">
```

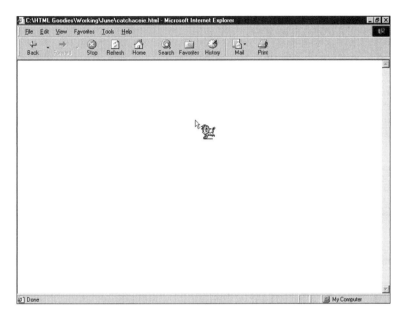

See the X and the Y setting denoting position on the entire browser screen (document.all)? That's the basic format.

You can get the same effect on Netscape Navigator with just a couple of changes.

Navigator Next

The effect is the same except that the players change a little bit. Here the author, Grab Bland, has set up a Layer and then attached it to the same X and Y location format.

Here's the code:

```
<SCRIPT LANGUAGE="javascript">
//(C) copyright 1998 greg bland all rights reserved
function trackit(ev) {
document.layers[0].pageX = ev.pageX
document.layers[0].pageY = ev.pageY
}
```

```
document.captureEvents(Event.MOUSEMOVE)
document.onMouseMove = trackit
</script>
<LAYER NAME="mymouse" BGCOLOR="white" TOP=100 left="100" z-index=0>
<IMG SRC="kittenrunning.gif">
</LAYER>
```

Fancy Trailing Stuff

This is the big trick, getting the effect to work the same across browsers. Yes, you can simply create a large script from the two smaller ones shown previously set up as a simple if/else format. If the browser is IE, write this script to the page. If it is Netscape Navigator, write the other to the page.

However, the trick that really moves people isn't only to get the mouse to be followed, it's to get the stuff that's following the mouse to, itself, do tricks. By that I mean, instead of a simply static following image, have the images that follow explode, wag like a tail, or multiply. That's where the real fun lies in having one of these on your page.

The vast majority of the mouse trail tricks I see come from a site called Dynamic Drive (http://www.dynamicdrive.com). You can link to the mouse trail page here: http://www.dynamicdrive.com/dynamicindex13/index.html. There are other places, and a quick search on Yahoo will pop them all up.

The trail effect on this page is by Philip Winston and can be found here: http://www.dynamicdrive.com/dynamicindex13/trailer2.htm.

It's a simple copy, paste, and download of a single image. The code is basically just what I showed you earlier except there are both divisions and elements that work on both browsers. In fact, except for the fancy coding that creates a sort of *gravity*, the codes are a lot like what I showed you previously.

There's not a whole lot more to tell. Now you understand the basic reason why the mouse trail works and how to get one on your own page. That's the easy part.

The hard part is deciding if the mouse trail is really an effect that adds to, or harms, your page.

Chapter 3

Neat Stuff with Text and Images

After you've mastered the advanced tricks with text and images alone, you can move on to manipulating them together. This chapter contains the following tutorials to help you dazzle your audience:

- Placing Text Over Images
- RevealTrans Filter
- Internet Explorer Text and Image Filters
- Internet Explorer Wave Filters
- Toggling Images and Text in Internet Explorer
- Toggling Netscape's Layers

Placing Text Over Images

Now and again I wonder if people are reading all the stuff I write. When I put up the last FAQ page at HTML Goodies, I answered a question from a reader about putting text over an image. She wanted to be able to put the name of the person in the picture on top of the picture, like a caption. I said that it couldn't be done without the use of a graphics editor. Well, KaBoom! The email poured in.

 You can find thistutorial, and all of its examples, online at http://www.htmlgoodies.com/ beyond/textonimages.html.

 You can download just the examples at http://www.htmlgoodies.com/wpg/.

Yes, people are reading. I will take the weasel road right now and say that when I answered the question, it was correct. Now the variables have changed right out from under me, and the version 4.0 browsers have offered a few different ways to do it. In this section, I'll outline three.

The Easiest Way I Know

Here you go. Figure 3.1 shows text over a stunning image of yours truly.

Figure 3.1
Hey, he's cute!

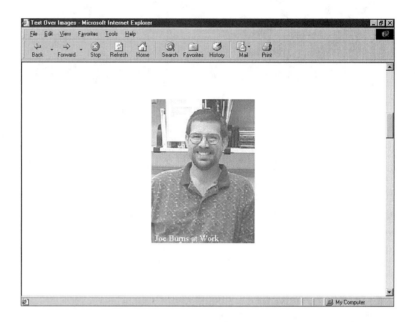

Like the haircut? Most of the top is gone, as well as most of the beard. I thought about getting a new character for the home page, but I still like the old one. Besides, as of the writing of this book, I'm back to a full head of hair and full beard. I go for the "mountain man" look once every couple of years.

Here is the code that created the caption:

```
<TABLE BORDER="0" cellpadding="0" CELLSPACING="0">
<TR>
<TD WIDTH="221" HEIGHT="300" BACKGROUND="newjoe01.jpg" VALIGN="bottom">
<FONT SIZE="+1" COLOR="yellow">Joe Burns at Work</FONT></TD>
</TR>
</TABLE>
```

I got the effect using a single table cell, adding a background, and then some text, like so:

- ⬤ `<TABLE BORDER="0" cellpadding="0" CELLSPACING="0">`—This is the format for the cell. You need to set everything to zero so that the cell borders lay right against the image. That way, you have better control over the text in relation to the image.

- ⬤ `<TR>`—This starts the table row.

- ⬤ `<TD WIDTH="221" HEIGHT="300" BACKGROUND="newjoe01.jpg" VALIGN="bottom">`—This is what does the trick. I set the image in Figure 3.1 as the background of the image cell. Note that I added the height and width of the image. **You need to do that**. If you don't, the cell will only conform to the size of the text you put after the `<TD>` command. In other words, you won't see the entire picture.

- ⬤ `<FONT SIZE="+1" COLOR="yellow">Joe Burns at Work</FONT></TD>`—This is the text that appears on the image. I used a `FONT` size and color command to get the text to show up a little better.

- ⬤ `</TR>`—This ends the table row.

- ⬤ `</TABLE>`—This ends the whole deal.

Doing It Through Layers

Although that table example is good enough, we at Goodies, Inc., go further and show you a couple of other methods. Here's a bit of code that performs pretty much the exact same thing (it's done with layers, so you have to be running Netscape 4.0 to see the effects):

```
<LAYER LEFT=250 TOP=500>
<IMG SRC=newjoe02.gif>
</LAYER>
<LAYER LEFT=250 TOP=500>
<IMG SRC=overtext.gif>
</LAYER>
```

See the commands in action in Figure 3.2.

Pretty nifty! That's my Paul McCartney, Sergeant Pepper pose—in case you didn't know.

As you can see, the effect is the same, but the parts are a little different. Look at the code. I set up two layers, but this time I did it with two images. One is of the back of my head (`newjoe02.jpg`), and the other is an image of the same size with the text "That Is Not a Bald Spot" written on it. Both are set to start 250 pixels from the left and 100 pixels from the top of the browser's window.

Remember that layers lay one over the top of the other in the order they are written. That's why the text image is written second.

Figure 3.2
Hey, he's... going bald.

The trick is that I made the image with the text transparent, except for the text itself. That way, the other image shows through and you get the effect.

It's a bit of work. But, if you are chopping up your pages using layers and DIV sections, this is the way to go about setting up the effect.

Why Not Position the Text?

Positioning the text is a capital idea. We're going to use the positioning commands available to Internet Explorer browsers to position the text and image so that one lays over the top of the other.

The idea is basically the same as with layers, except that you don't have to create the text image like you did previously. Figure 3.3 shows the effect.

Here's the code:

```
<IMG SRC="newjoe03.jpg">
<DIV STYLE="position:absolute; top:250px; left:20px; width:200px; height:25px">
<CENTER><FONT SIZE="+2" COLOR="00ff00">Looking Into The Future</FONT></CENTER>
</DIV>
```

That DIV section should really be all on one line.

I'm looking in to my computer screen actually. It's a bad shot. It looks like I should have a county jail number card underneath my face.

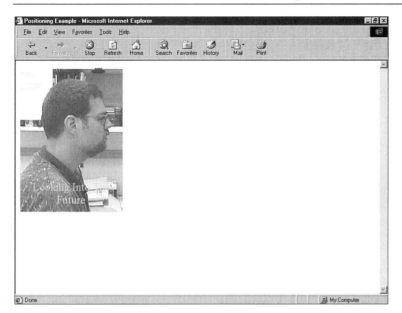

Figure 3.3
Hey, he's ignoring me.

The image is just sitting where it would normally sit. The text, formatted to +2 font size and a green color, has been placed in a division. Style Sheet commands then place it 250 pixels from the top of the browser window and 20 pixels from the left side. The height and width command set the height and width of the division the text will sit inside. You shouldn't set that any wider than the image. That way, you'll lessen your chance of rolling the text over the sides.

Most of you will probably end up using the TABLE background method up top, but maybe not. So now you can set your images with as many words of wisdom as you can muster. I haven't any at the moment.

RevealTrans **Filter**

First Things First: This is a DHTML event; thus you must be running MSIE4.0+ to see the effect. However, browsers that do not understand DHTML will happily ignore the commands without throwing errors, so feel free to use them at will.

 You can find this tutorial, and all of its examples, online at http://www.htmlgoodies.com/ *beyond*/revealTransFilter.html.

 You can download just the examples at http://www.htmlgoodies.com/wpg/.

Do you want a cool effect? Dig this! Figure 3.4 shows what this tutorial teaches you. Notice that the button says to click it for the image to go away. I clicked it and then captured the image as the image was disappearing. Inside of two seconds, it was gone. Really!

Figure 3.4
No eggs, thanks...

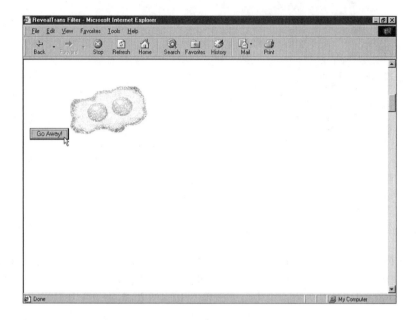

Better yet, you can also set it so that the image comes back.

What you're seeing there is the revealTrans() filter at work. Two separate JavaScripts are using the filter to make a SPAN disappear and then reappear. I'll show you the first one and then explain the second one, but only quickly. (It's just like the first one only backward.)

Make It Disappear

As I said previously, the image, "eggs.gif", itself doesn't disappear. The SPAN surrounding the image disappears. The image just goes with it. So, let's start with the SPAN and its image. The code looks like this:

```
<INPUT TYPE="button" VALUE="Go Away!" onClick="go();">
<SPAN ID=Egg1 Style="Visibility:visible;
Filter:revealTrans(duration=2);width:179;height:110">
<IMG SRC="eggs.gif">
</SPAN>
```

The first line is a form button with the text "Go Away!" The button is there to act as a trigger for the function "go()". When clicked, the function fires.

The code is a basic SPAN surrounding the image flag displaying the eggs.gif. A NAME, Egg1, is given to the SPAN. That links it to the next JavaScript covered in the next paragraph. Also, inside the SPAN are some Style Sheet commands and the filter. Note that the visibility of the SPAN is set to "visible". That changes in the next script. Then comes the Filter:revealTrans(duration=2). You can probably guess that the 2 means two seconds for the effect. Then the height and width of the image are given so that the SPAN fits it perfectly.

Okay. Got the SPAN? Good. Now here is the script that does the dirty work:

```
<SCRIPT LANGUAGE="javascript">
function go() {
Egg1.filters[0].Apply();
if (Egg1.style.visibility == "visible")
{
Egg1.style.visibility = "hidden";
Egg1.filters.revealTrans.transition=12;
}
else
{
Egg1.style.visibility = "visible";
Egg1.filters[0].transition=12;
}
Egg1.filters[0].Play();
}
</SCRIPT>
```

The script is pretty straightforward. When the function go() is triggered, the filter in Egg1 is applied. Remember that Egg1 is the SPAN. We gave it that name in the first script.

Then, if Egg1 is visible, set its value to "hidden" using transition number 12. Otherwise, make the SPAN Egg1 visible by using transition number 12.

Then play the transition! There's nothing to it!

Transition Numbers

There are 22 different transitions to choose from. There is also transition 23, which chooses a number at random. I just happen to like 12.

And no, you do not need both transitions set to 12. It can be two different numbers. Table 3.1 describes the magic 23 numbers.

Table 3.1   Transition Effects

Number	What Happens
1	Reveals from inside out
2	Scrolls in from outer parts
3	Scrolls out from the center
4	Scrolls up from the button
5	Scrolls down from the top
6	Scrolls left to the right
7	Scrolls right to the left
8	Displays vertical blinds left to right
9	Displays horizontal blinds top to bottom
10	Displays a combination of 8 and 9
11	Looks a lot like 8
12	Comes in, in pixels
13	Scrolls in from outer parts
14	Scrolls out from the center
15	Closes from both the top and bottom
16	Opens from center to top and bottom
17	Displays a diagonal roll from right to left
18	Displays a different angle diagonal roll right to left
19	Displays number 17 the other way
20	Displays number 18 the other way
21	Displays random horizontal lines
22	Displays random vertical lines
23	Displays completely random

After Transition 23, the cycle of effects appears to start over. Any one will work just fine. Some are just more interesting than others.

Make It Go Away

There are really two things to discuss when it comes to reversing the effect: simply setting the current script to go the opposite way and putting a second `revealTrans()` on a page.

If all you want to do is make the script and SPAN previously noted to go from invisible to visible, it's simple. Everywhere you see the word `"visible"`, you change it to `"hidden"`; and everywhere you see the word `"hidden"`, you change it to `"visible"`. Don't forget to change the instance in the SPAN as well.

But what if you want to put a second `revealTrans()` on the same page? You can, but you need to do two things.

First, you need to set a new function name in the script. I chose `goAway()` for my second function name. Then you need to update that name in the Form Button `onClick` Event Handler.

Then there's the `NAME=` in the `SPAN`. Remember how we named the `SPAN` in the original script `Egg1`? Well, that `NAME` connected the `SPAN` and the JavaScript. This means that if you put another `revealTrans()` on a page, the first name is dead and cannot be used by anything else. Thus, you have to change the name of the `SPAN` and each time that name appears in the script.

Here's a hint to do it quickly: Copy the script and previous `SPAN` on to a separate text editor, like WordPad or SimpleText. Then, choose Replace from the Edit menu. Type in the current name of the `SPAN` and then what you would like the new name to be and choose to Replace All. Bingo! It's done.

Now you can copy the new script and `SPAN` and paste it wherever you want it. No sweat! That's what I had to do here. I went with the name `Egg2`. Clever, huh?

The following code is the second script and `SPAN` from before. It has a new function name, a new `NAME` for the `SPAN`—which has also been changed throughout the script—and is set to go in the opposite direction of the first `revealTrans()`. The transitions are still set to 12, though. I really do like that number:

```
<SCRIPT LANGUAGE="javascript">
function goAgain()
{
Egg2.filters[0].Apply();
if (Egg2.style.visibility == "hidden")
{
Egg2.style.visibility = "visible";
Egg2.filters.revealTrans.transition=12;
}
else {
Egg2.style.visibility = "hidden";
Egg2.filters[0].transition=12;
}
Egg2.filters[0].Play();
}
</SCRIPT>
<INPUT TYPE=button VALUE="Lemme See It" onClick="goAgain();">
<SPAN ID=Egg2 Style="Visibility:hidden;
Filter:revealTrans(duration=2);width:179;height:110"> <IMG SRC="eggs.gif">
</SPAN>
```

No Button

As you can probably tell, using a button to start the effect is not very useful. Just remember that as long as the effect can be surrounded by a SPAN and an Event Handler is used to trigger the function, this can be triggered any number of ways. An onLoad Event Handler can trigger the effect when the page loads. You could also set the effect to trigger using an onMouseOver as illustrated in Figure 3.5.

Figure 3.5
See the text "Thank You!" coming in?

By the way, I got the effect to occur in less than a second by setting the duration to .25. Faster than that seemed to kill the effect.

Internet Explorer Text and Image Filters

First Things First: The material covered in this tutorial is only compatible with MSIE browsers versions 4.0 and above. Feel free to use them, though; browsers that do not comprehend the commands will happily ignore them.

 You can find this tutorial, and all of its examples, online at http://www.htmlgoodies.com/ beyond/textfilter.html.

 You can download just the examples at http://www.htmlgoodies.com/wpg/.

I often get questions from people asking how someone got a great font or neat text layout. I usually found that the text was an image. Well, now you have some limited ability to play around with text layout and appearance through Microsoft filters. They work like Style Sheet commands and give some great effects.

Using the Filter

You can use filters just like Style Sheet commands. You can affect just one element in this format:

```
<SPAN STYLE="width:200;height:30;filter:fliph()">Affected Text</SPAN>
```

This format also works to affect images:

```
<DIV STYLE="width:200;height:30;filter:fliph()">
<IMG SRC="eggs.gif">
</DIV>
```

Please Note: Parentheses follow the filter name. In those parentheses, you'll be able to manipulate the filter's strength, color, and direction.

Please also note this. See the "width" and "height" settings? You need to denote at least the width so that this filter has something to act on. If you do not supply that parameter, the filter will not run. That includes both text and images.

Multiple Elements

I would assume that you'd use these commands mainly in the preceding format because a height or width must be set each time. However, you can also use the filters by assigning them to one type of text, say a hypertext link, or all images, through a Style block like so:

```
<STYLE TYPE="text/css">
 A {width:200;height:50;filter:blur(Direction=90)}
 IMG {width:200;height:50;filter:shadow(color=red)}
</STYLE>
```

Now, every link carries the blur filter coming straight in from the right, and every image carries a red shadow. That makes for an ugly page, huh?

Filter Examples

The quickest way of showing you these filters is to just run them down. You'll see the effect on both text and an image. They both normally look like Figure 3.6.

Figure 3.6
Text and eggs? Great—breakfast!

Here's the code that rendered Figure 3.6:

```
<DIV STYLE="background:#ffffcc;width:200;height:30">
<FONT SIZE=+1>Here's What You Get.</FONT>
</DIV>
```

I made the text a little bigger and gave the background some color to show height and width. Remember that the filter is stuck in at the end of the run of Style Sheet commands just like I showed previously. Here we go. Enjoy.

Filter Name	*Code*	*Image*	
Horizontal Flip	`filter:fliph()`	.teƆ uoY tahW s'ereH	**Figure 3.7** *Flip...*
Vertical Flip	`filter:flipv()`	Here's What You Get.	**Figure 3.8** *Upside down.*

Filter Name	*Code*	*Image*	
Invert	`filter:invert()`	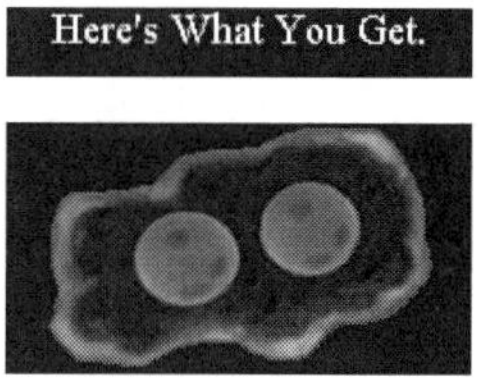	**Figure 3.9** *That's spooky, huh?*
Gray Scale	`filter:gray()`	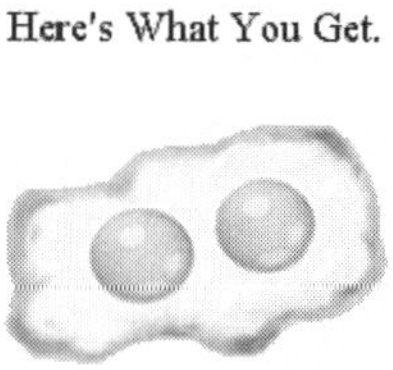	**Figure 3.10** *I'm just showing a little gray. I can cover it.*
X-Ray	`filter:xray()`	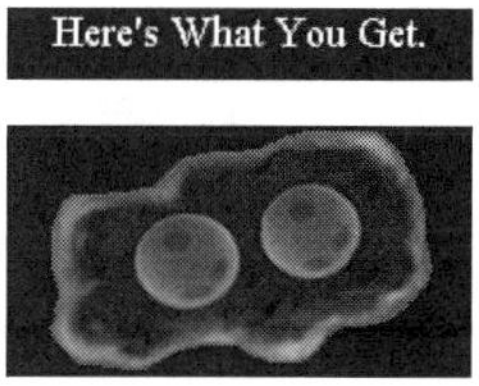	**Figure 3.11** *Eggs don't have bones…*
Mask	`filter:mask()`		**Figure 3.12** *Uhhh…where did it go? That's the point actually.*
Blur	`filter:blur (Strength=#, Direction=##)`		**Figure 3.13** *Take me home. I'm seeing double eggs.*

Filter Name	**Code**	**Image**	

Shadow	`filter:shadow`
	`(Color=##,`
	`Direction=##)`
		 Here's What You Get.	**Figure 3.14**
			It knows...

Drop Shadow	`filter:dropshadow`
	`(Color=#,`
	`Direction=#)`
		 Here's What You Get.	**Figure 3.15**
			It knows too, I guess.

Glow	`filter:glow`
	`(Color=##,`
	`Strength=#)`
		 Here's What You Get.	**Figure 3.16**
			Sir, your eggs are glowing.

Set the Strength number higher for more blur. The direction can be set to come from any one of the following. (If you do not set a direction, the blur will come from 270 by default.)

0—Top

45—Top right

90—Bottom

135—Bottom right

180—Bottom

225—Bottom left

270—Left

315—Top left

Set the color to a word color code. If you use a hex code, make sure that you use a leading pound sign (#). The direction of the shadow can be set to come from any one of the following. (If you do not set a direction, the shadow will come from 270 by default.)

> 0—Top
>
> 45—Top right
>
> 90—Bottom
>
> 135—Bottom right
>
> 180—Bottom
>
> 225—Bottom left
>
> 270—Left
>
> 315—Top left

Set the color to a word color code. If you use a hex code, make sure that you use a leading pound sign (#). The direction of the shadow can be set to come from any one of the following. (If you do not set a direction, the shadow will come from 270 by default.)

> 0—Top
>
> 45—Top right
>
> 90—Bottom
>
> 135—Bottom right
>
> 180—Bottom
>
> 225—Bottom left
>
> 270—Left
>
> 315—Top left

The property is read/write with a default value of 270.

Set the color to a word color code. If you use a hex code, make sure that you use a leading pound sign (#). Set the Strength number higher for more glow, smaller for less.

Internet Explorer Wave Filters

The Wave Filter is a great effect that will wave either text or an image, as long as that text or image sits inside of a division or SPAN.

You can find this tutorial, and all of its examples, online at http://www.htmlgoodies.com/ beyond/wavefilter.html.

 You can download just the examples at http://www.htmlgoodies.com/wpg/.

The Wave Filter acts a lot like a Style Sheet command, as do the other static text filters. I just broke this one out from the other text filters because there are so many more settings to play with.

Examples

Let me give you an example of what this filter can do. Take this code... please:

```
<DIV STYLE="width:350;height:70;filter:wave(strength=4, freq=2,
lightstrength=40, add=0, phase=20)">
<FONT SIZE=+3>Here's What You Get.</FONT>
</DIV>
```

It gives you the effect shown in Figure 3.17.

Figure 3.17
Ooooo! Wavy gravey.

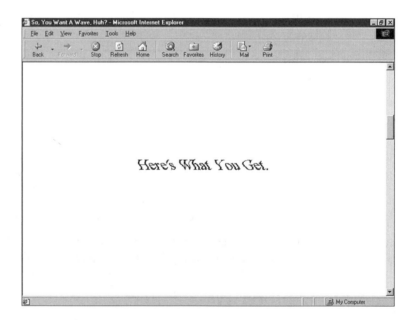

Now, let's apply the same parameters to an image. The code looks like this:

```
<DIV STYLE="width:350;height:70;filter:wave(strength=4, freq=2,
lightstrength=40, add=0, phase=120)">
<IMG SRC="/images/eggs.gif">
</DIV>
```

...and it gives you Figure 3.18.

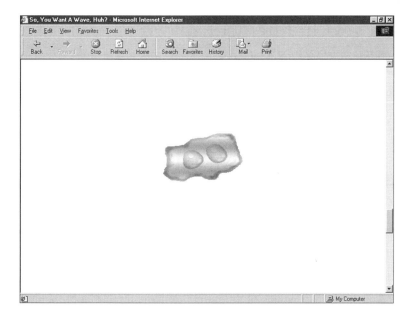

Figure 3.18
Ooooo! Wavy eggey.

Make a point of keeping all the Style Sheet and parameter codes in the <DIV> on the same line. If you don't, you might not get the effect.

Parameters

The real fun of this filter is setting the parameters to differing levels of intensity. Go nuts! Here's what each one means and how you can set it—just follow the format in the previous code examples:

- ● add   Do you want the original image added to the mix? Use 0 for no and 1 for yes.
- ● enabled   Is the effect turned on or not? Use 0 for no and 1 for yes.
- ● freq   How many waves do you want?
- ● lightStrength   How much light intensity do you want?

● phase   At what phase do you want the waving to begin? If you try different numbers, you'll set the difference.

● strength   How strong do you want the filter? Again, higher numbers are stronger.

Keep in mind that this effect only works on IE browsers 4.0 or better, but feel free to use the commands regardless. Browsers that do not understand the commands will happily ignore them.

Toggling Images and Text in Internet Explorer

First Things First: This is a tutorial dealing with DHTML. You need to be running an Internet Explorer browser, 4.0 level or better, to see the effect.

 You can find this tutorial, and all of its examples, online at `http://www.htmlgoodies.com/beyond/toggle.html`.

 You can download just the examples at `http://www.htmlgoodies.com/wpg/`.

This tutorial is basically a DHTML session. What I'm going to show you here is how to make a division appear and disappear in MSIE. I also have a sister tutorial to this one that teaches you how to make a layer appear and disappear in Netscape Navigator. It's covered in the next section, "Toggling Netscape's Layers." The effect is the same, but all the commands that do the trick are different, so multiple companies have a hand in the process. Basically, this means that I'm about to get a bunch of letters that tell me that this effect is actually called "visibility", "layering," or "Steve."

The truth is because the MSIE and Navigator browsers are moving in such different directions, it's hard to create one definitive statement that covers the effect. In one of my computer books, the author refers to making a layer appear and disappear as "toggling." I thought was as good a term as any.

But no matter what you name it—the effect will still be as sweet (to paraphrase Bill Shakespeare—I'm a cultured man you know).

Toggling with MSIE

In Microsoft Internet Explorer, you get the effect through DHTML commands. Now remember that these commands are only supported in IE 4.0 and above and are not supported in Navigator (as of 10/20/01). So when you set up this effect, make sure that the users are running IE 4 or better. You can do that through setting up a browser detect script.

If you don't, errors fly all over the place. This is a good one to make sure that your people are prepared for.

Look carefully at Figures 3.19–3.21. The effects are demonstrated here.

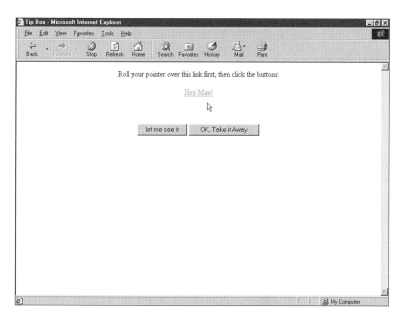

Figure 3.19
Notice that my pointer is off the text "Hey Man!".

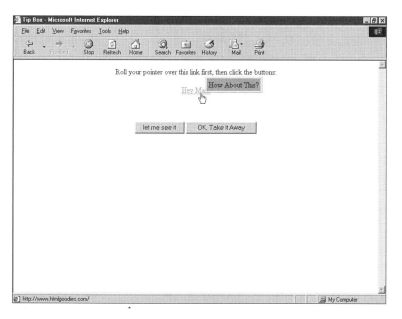

Figure 3.20
Now the pointer is on top of the text, and the box popped up.

Figure 3.21
I've gotten the box to pop up now by using the button. Notice that the other button will take it away.

It's not that difficult of an effect either. Basically what's happening is that I have positioned a division on the page. In that division, I put a table cell with the words "How About This?" inside, but just about anything can be put in the division.

Here's the entire script (I break it apart just after the listing):

```
<script language="JavaScript">
function ShowIt()
{
document.body.insertAdjacentHTML('BeforeEnd',
➥'<DIV STYLE="position:absolute; TOP:35px; LEFT:410px"
➥ID="TheTip"><TABLE BORDER="1" CELLPADDING="3">
➥<TD BGCOLOR="ff00ff">How About This?</TD></TABLE></DIV>');
}
function LoseIt()
{
TheTip.innerHTML = " ";
TheTip.outerHTML = " ";
}
</script>
<center><a href="http://www.htmlgoodies.com" onMouseOver="ShowIt()"
➥onMouseOut="LoseIt()">Hey Man!</A>
</center>
<P> <P>
<FORM>
```

```
<INPUT TYPE="button" Value="let me See It" onClick="ShowIt()">
<INPUT TYPE="button" Value="OK, Take It Away" onClick="LoseIt()">
</FORM>
```

Make the Division Appear

After the division was created, I encased it in a JavaScript function so that I could call on it whenever it is clicked or moused over.

Next, I set up another JavaScript function so that when the mouse moved off the link, the division disappeared again.

After I have a function set up that makes the division appear and disappear, the process is simple. Call the correct function, and the effect comes to life. Well, it's relatively simple anyway.

Make It Appear

The harder of the two functions is the one that makes the division appear, so we'll start with that one. It goes up in between the <HEAD> flags and it looks like this:

```
<SCRIPT LANGUAGE="javascript">
function ShowIt()
{
document.body.insertAdjacentHTML('BeforeEnd',
➡'<DIV STYLE="position:absolute; TOP:35px;
➡LEFT:410px" ID="TheTip"> <TABLE BORDER="1" CELLPADDING="3">
➡<TD BGCOLOR="ff00ff">How About This?</TD></TABLE></DIV>');
}
</SCRIPT>
```

That one line is pretty long, huh? Yeah. It can be broken down, if you really want, into multiple document.write statements, but why? It's just more typing for the same effect.

So, what does it do? Nothing. It won't do anything until it's called on by its function name later in the page. Let's tear it apart even more.

This is a JavaScript, so we have to start with the familiar "SCRIPT LANGUAGE=" flag.

The function is named ShowIt(). Note that fancy brackets always surround the JavaScript commands making up the event that the function performs.

Now here's the magic—we begin with a hierarchy statement that uses commands which are proprietary to MSIE. That's a nice way of saying that only Explorer understands them. It's DHTML.

69

`document.body.insertAdjacentHTML` represents to the IE browser that whatever follows is to go on the document, in the body, and what follows in parentheses is to be inserted as HTML.

In case you're wondering, and I know you are, there's also the command, `insertAdjacentText`. It works the same way except that it handles what appears in the following parentheses as text alone and does not compile it into HTML.

Inside the parentheses, the first command deals with where this little division should display in terms of the command that is calling for it. It doesn't come into play much in this scenario because we are calling on this division from a function and not from inside of an HTML command. But you still need to put something in there to denote where the inserted HTML will appear, or the format throws an error.

`'BeforeEnd'` means that the division should appear at the end of the element before the end tag. There are actually three others you can play with if you take this format and embed it in to an HTML flag:

- `BeforeBegin`—The item is inserted in front of the flag.
- `AfterBegin`—The item is inserted after the flag, but before the text.
- `AfterEnd`—The items is inserted after the end tag.

Now we get to the element that will be inserted. It's a division that has been positioned and given the `NAME` `"TheTip"` so that we can call on it later. It looks like this:

```
<DIV STYLE="position:absolute; TOP:35px; LEFT:410px" ID="TheTip">
```

In terms of the effect, the positioning is very important. If you decide to have multiple divisions popping up over a series of links, you need to have each one positioned so that they pop up at the right place.

Or, as I've seen it done, have them all appear in the exact same place, which is a great effect. One just lays right over the other. It's like a little billboard popping up.

You know what I've found with positioning? It's best to be most concerned with the pixels from the top and go real easy on the pixels from the left. Also, go easy on the concept of *absolute positioning*. There are too many screen resolutions and sizes out there to be overly concerned. Use the command `positioning:absolute`, but keep in mind that you're only going to get "pretty close" positioning. It'll keep your blood pressure down.

What follows in the division is a basic one-celled table with a purple background. It might look a little strange because it is all on one line, but that's all it is.

The `</DIV>` flag kills the line of text.

The second curly bracket and the `</SCRIPT>` wrap up the entire format.

Now take that function, stick it in between `<SCRIPT LANGUAGE="javascript">` and `</SCRIPT>` commands, and put that between the `<HEAD>` flags. So now, you understand and posses a function that will make the division appear. But can you make it disappear again? Read on to find out how.

Make the Division Disappear

What we need to do is set up another function.

```
function LoseIt()
{
TheTip.innerHTML = " ";
TheTip.outerHTML = " ";
}
```

This one's pretty easy to figure out even if DHTML is brand new to you. The function, named `LoseIt()`, simply sets two sections of the division to represent nothing. In other words, it disappears.

Remember, the name of the division is `"TheTip"`. Go ahead and look at the "appear" function again if you missed that point. It's important. In this function, we set two parameters, `innerHTML` and `outerHTML`, to nothing. Note that the quote marks contain only an empty space. The end. There's no more visible division. That's very clever.

Now, take that code, stick it between `<SCRIPT LANGUAGE="javascript">` and `</SCRIPT>` commands, and put that in between the `<HEAD>` flags.

OK, now we're set. We can call for the division in the first function any darn time we feel like it.

Call for the Division

Now that we have the two functions just waiting to be used, we can call for them as we would any other function. In the two examples shown in this tutorial, I set up a rollover on a hypertext link and also made the division appear through the use of a form button. Here's the code for each.

The Hypertext Link:

```
<A HREF="http://www.htmlgoodies.com"
onMouseOver="ShowIt()" onMouseOut="LoseIt()">Hey Man!</A>
```

The Form Buttons

```
<FORM>
<INPUT TYPE="button" Value="let me see it" onClick="ShowIt()">
<INPUT TYPE="button" Value="OK, Take it Away" onClick="LoseIt()">
</FORM>
```

There's no real science to it. I've called for the functions through basic onMouseOver, onMouseOut, and onClick Event Handlers depending on how the user would get the effect.

More Divisions

This is a great effect if you have a series of links down one side of the page. The effect of multiple divisions appearing one after the other looks high-tech and appears interactive.

The only downfall, if you want to call it that, is that each of these divisions is an element in its own right. They each have a NAME attribute assigned. Thus, you need to create a totally new function to make the division appear and disappear.

For example, let's say that you already have the division described in this tutorial installed on a page. You want a second one. Here's what you need to do:

Create a whole new function that makes the division appear. The easiest method would be to copy and paste the current "appear" function and change its name. The current appear function is named ShowIt(). You could simply change the name to ShowIt2().

You need to go in to the division itself and change out:

- The TOP and LEFT positioning pixels
- The NAME of the division
- What is contained in the division

Finally, copy and paste the function that makes the first one disappear. Again, you need to make a few changes:

- You need to change the name of the function. The current function is named LoseIt(). You could simply change the new function name to LoseIt2().
- You need to change the NAME element of the innerHTML and outerHTML statements. Remember that they are currently attached to the first division named "TheTip".
- You need to change "TheTip" to whatever you named this new division.

Now you're good to go with a second division. Yes, it's a little work, but the results are great.

A Final Note

While working on this tutorial, I played with multiple and single divisions. I can honestly say that what makes these things really shine is the positioning element. Where they pop up is really the point of all this, more so than the fact that they pop up at all. I found that you couldn't be overly precise. Get close. I loved the look of an element on the left side of the page popping a window on the right.

Got it? Great! Now learn how to toggle with Netscape's Layers.

Toggling Netscape's Layers

First Things First: This is a tutorial dealing with Netscape Layers. You need to be running a Navigator browser, 4.0 level or better, to see the effect.

 You can find this tutorial, and all of its examples, online at `http://www.htmlgoodies.com/beyond/toggle2.html.`

 You can download just the examples at `http://www.htmlgoodies.com/wpg/.`

This tutorial is one of a pair that offers the same effect, but uses totally different methods to get the job done. If you haven't already, you should take the time to read over this tutorial's twin, "Toggling with MSIE." The toggling effect, an item being made able to appear and disappear, is done in MSIE by using a division. In this Netscape-based tutorial, we'll get the same effect by getting a layer to toggle.

If you have read the other tutorial, I think you'll find that this one is a whole lot easier to understand.

The Effect

Figures 3.22–3.24 illustrate the effect. You'll recognize it from the tutorial just before this one. Remember to pay close attention to the differences in the figures to really understand what's happening.

Here is the full code—I'll break it down as the tutorial goes on:

```
<LAYER NAME="layer1" visibility=hide bgcolor="ff00ff"
➥WIDTH="100" HEIGHT="100" TOP="75" LEFT="450">
➥<center><br><br>Ta Da!</center></LAYER>
<A HREF="www.htmlgoodies.com" onMouseOver="document.layer1.visibility='show'"
onMouseOut="document.layer1.visibility='hide'">Go to Goodies</A>
<FORM>
<INPUT TYPE="button" VALUE="Let Me See It"
➥onClick="document.layer1.visibility='show'">
```

```
<INPUT TYPE="button" VALUE="Take It Away"
➥onClick="document.layer1.visibility='hide'">
</FORM>
```

Figure 3.22
Notice my pointer is off the text "Go to Goodies."

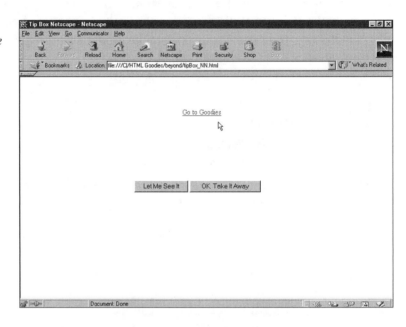

Figure 3.23
Now the pointer is on top of the text, and the box popped up.

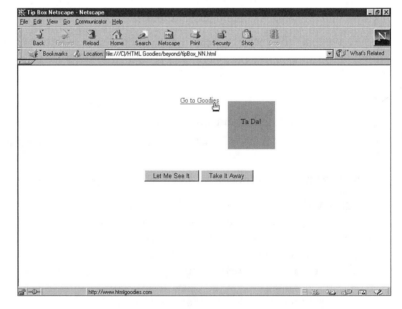

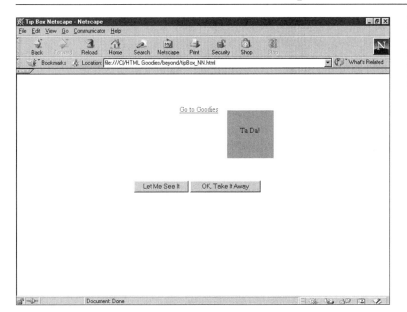

Figure 3.24
I've gotten the box to pop up now by using the button. Notice that the other button will take it away.

The Layer

The layer itself carries with it all the stuff needed to place it and make it disappear. It's a one trick pony, but it turns that trick so well as emphasized here:

```
<LAYER NAME="layer1" VISIBILITY="hide" BGCOLOR="ff00ff"
WIDTH="100" HEIGHT="100" TOP="105" LEFT="450">Ta Da!
</LAYER>
```

If you haven't noticed already, dig that VISIBILITY="hide". That's what makes the layer invisible. VISIBILITY="hide" hides the layer.

All I've got in the layer is a background set to purple and the words Ta Da!. I'm a clever fellow.

The other parts I'm interested in pointing out to you are the TOP and LEFT settings. It's my opinion that this effect literally hinges on the correct positioning of the layer. I've seen the effect so that each layer comes up near the element it is supposed to work with, and I've seen the effect in which the layer comes up somewhere far away from the element that caused it to appear. I also like the look of multiple layers popping up and disappearing due to multiple mouse rollovers. However, each layer popped up in the exact same place. It was like a billboard. It looked great. So when you set this up for yourself, remember that positioning is king.

I also wanted to make sure that you saw that the layer was given a name. In this case, it's layer1. I again made the name up all by myself.

You'll also note that there's an end layer flag. You need that.

Actually now that I've looked over the text, heck, I've pointed out just about everything. Eh, it'll help you later.

Getting the Toggle Effect

The entire effect revolves around a JavaScript hierarchy statement meant to point an Event Handler right at the layer in question. Remember, the layer has a name, layer1. Later we'll talk about getting multiple layer toggles. Then the name of the layer becomes quite important.

Here's the code that made up the first hypertext link in the example:

```
<A HREF="www.htmlgoodies.com"
onMouseOver="document.layer1.visibility='show'"
onMouseOut="document.layer1.visibility='hide'">Go to Goodies</A>
```

This is the JavaScript hierarchy statement that makes the magic:

```
document.layer1.visibility='show'
```

And here's its counterpart:

```
document.layer1.visibility='hide'
```

The first makes the layer visible. The second makes the layer disappear. Notice that the code is very similar to the code used in an image flip. An onMouseOver and onMouseOut Event Handler is used to enact the hierarchy statement. When the mouse passes over, the layer appears. When the mouse moves off, the layer is hidden. It's just like magic except without the seven beautiful assistants and the disappearing tiger.

The Button Code

As you probably noticed, there are also two form buttons that get the effect. They work the same way incorporating the hierarchy statements, except the buttons use an onClick handler to get the job done. Here's the basic code:

```
<FORM>
<INPUT TYPE="button" VALUE="Let Me See It"
➥onClick="document.layer1.visibility='show'">
<INPUT TYPE="button" VALUE="Take It Away"
```

```
➥onClick="document.layer1.visibility='hide'">
</FORM>
```

Multiple Toggling Layers

As promised, let's talk about toggling multiple layers. Imagine a long line of links down the left side of a page. It would look great if you could get a new layer to show up every time the mouse passed over the next link. It would look like a glorified series of image flips.

The effect is not hard, but it does require some attention. You'll obviously have to create a new layer code for each layer you want to pop up. I would assume that they're all probably going to say different things.

You'll need to set new TOP and LEFT positions unless you want all the layers to appear in the same location (which isn't a bad look actually).

But most of all, you will have to assign each layer a different name. They cannot all have the same name. Think up new names for each layer! (Did that drive the point home?)

Now, after you have new names for each layer, you can create a JavaScript hierarchy for each individual layer. If you have a layer named bob, you would use the hierarchy statements:

```
document.bob.visibility='show'
```

and

```
document.bob.visibility='hide'
```

to affect that bob layer.

Now imagine that you create a second layer named george. The hierarchy statement you created for bob will not work for george. You need to use new george-ready hierarchy statements. They'll look like this:

```
document.george.visibility='show'
```

and

```
document.george.visibility='hide'
```

Every time you create a new layer, you need to create new hierarchy statements. Then you can set links and buttons to toggle just the right layer.

And how much fun will that be?

Chapter 4

What About the Page's Design?

Site design plays a key role in any Web page. How your page looks—its organization, layout, blocking—everything impacts the viewer in a certain way. This chapter includes some tips on how to better your site's presentation and make users come back for more. Tips and tricks included in this chapter are as follows:

- Dynamic Fonts
- No Borders!
- Post by Screen Size
- Internal Browser Test
- No Selection Rectangle in IE
- Resize Your Browser Window
- Printable Pages
- Rounded Corners in Tables
- Full Screen Effect
- Pop-Under Windows
- New Window: No TITLE Bar

Dynamic Fonts

I get questions on the discussion groups and my email asking how to change fonts on pages. Until recently, the only way was to use the FONT FACE= format and set it that way. The problem was that for the user to "see" the font, that font had to be installed on his computer.

Many people went to a font download site, grabbed some strange looking letters, and installed them on their computers. They then created pages using that font. The pages looked great until someone else tried to look at it. Because the second person didn't have the font installed on his computer—the text was plain.

I have seen pages that offer fonts as downloads so that the pages can be viewed correctly. That's much the same as suggesting users switch to a screen resolution different from their current settings. Very few people actually stop, change the screen settings, and then reenter the page. The same thing happens with fonts. My guess is that very few are downloaded and installed.

But what if you could offer the font behind the scenes? What if the font was simply a file that would download along with everything else? Then, the text would display correctly on all computers. Well, with some exceptions, you can do that right now.

 You can find this tutorial, and all of its examples, online at http://www.htmlgoodies.com/ beyond/dynamicfonts.html.

 You can download just the examples at http://www.htmlgoodies.com/wpg/.

Dynamic Fonts

Dynamic fonts are font style files that download along with the page that uses them. Think of them like an image—it's the same basic concept.

When you use these fonts, the font file downloads into your cache just like an image. Once there, as long as you don't clear your cache completely, the font will be there for all future visits. It is fun to watch the page the first time you use these fonts. The page comes in fully with the text in the default format. Then, after the font, or fonts, download, the entire page reloads and comes to life. It's a great effect.

The use of these fonts is basically a Netscape Navigator 4.0 or better feature right now. Internet Explorer does allow users to download an ActiveX element to see the fonts, but that means a gray box popping up when people try to use this format with IE. If the users click Yes, all is well.

If not, no dynamic font appears. Sorry!

PFR Fonts

Now, before you run out to your local font download site, remember that nothing on the Web is quite as easy as it sounds at first. Yes, you can use a dynamic font, but only a certain type of dynamic font. The font has to be in a format known as Portable Font Resource, or PFR. You'll know a font is in that format because the extension will be `.pfr`.

The next question is most likely, "Where do I get these things?" I found a few places, but not a lot. Maybe I just didn't search with the correct key words, but I didn't find a vast number of places offering the fonts. Here are those that did seem helpful:

> True Doc is the King Daddy of everything for these fonts. They have downloads, help files, and more info than you probably care to read.
> `http://www.truedoc.com`

> Bitstream World of Fonts: Good site, but the fonts require an outlay of cash.
> `http://www.bitstream.com/categories/products/index.html`

> VietPage Fonts: Ditto. `http://www.vietpage.com/dynamicfonts.html`

Of course, searching any of the major search engines should help turn up some fonts and font sites that might also be helpful.

The majority of the fonts I found were made available as long as you always had the font grabbed from the server offering them. Yes, it's pretty easy to download the font and run it from your own server, but these people are nice enough to offer these fonts: You should do what they ask. The effect is the same as if you were running it from your own server.

The next question is then—how do I make my own fonts? Well, from everything I've read, you have to grab a program specifically set to create fonts. A couple of the shareware programs did not have the capability to save in `pfr` format. If you have a pay-for program that creates fonts, check to see if it has the capability to save in `pfr`. If not, the people at `http://www.truedoc.com` suggest HexMac Typograph and Extensis BeyondPress.

I ran across an article suggesting that CorelDRAW has the capability to save fonts as `pfr`s.

If you do make your own fonts, here are the symbols you must create:

```
abcdefghijklmnopqrstuvwxyz

ABCDEFGHIJKLMNOPQRSTUVWXYZ

0123456789 &$?!%
```

Get the Font

Let's say that you've traveled to `http://www.truedoc.com` and have found a few fonts you like. I actually like three that they offer:

Amelia

AmeriGarmnd

BakerSignet

The preceding font names should be in the font suggested by the name. If not, your browser version might not be high enough, or the fonts might still be downloading (I'm grabbing three). By now though, they should be up and running.

In order to use a font, you need to grab it and download it into your browser's cache. You do that through LINK flags set in the document's HEAD flags. I grabbed three fonts, so the flags looked like this:

```
<LINK REL="FONTDEF" SRC="http://www.truedoc.com/pfrs/Amelia.pfr">
<LINK REL="FONTDEF" SRC="http://www.truedoc.com/pfrs/AmeriGarmnd.pfr">
<LINK REL="FONTDEF" SRC="http://www.truedoc.com/pfrs/BakerSignet.pfr">
<SCRIPT LANGUAGE="JavaScript" SRC="http://www.truedoc.com/activex/
➥tdserver.js">
</SCRIPT>
```

Notice that each font is being grabbed from the TrueDoc server, as they asked I do. If you use a font that is coming right from your own server, there is no need for the full URL.

Let's take a look at the code:

- ○ LINK sets up a link to something.
- ○ REL is the relation of the link to the document.
- ○ FONTDEF tells the document that this is a font definition.
- ○ SRC tells the browser where to get the font.
- ○ The URL is the path.

This is very important! The names of fonts are case sensitive. Uppercase letters have to stay that way.

Yes, but what about this:

```
<SCRIPT LANGUAGE="JavaScript" SRC="http://www.truedoc.com/activex/
➥tdserver.js">
</SCRIPT>
```

Remember I said previously in the section that in order for this to work on MSIE, you would need an ActiveX program. This is it. It's 68KB, and it has to be offered if MSIE users are to get in the game. By doing it this way, you are basically completing a step for the user. Microsoft offers a plug-in of its own at its MSIE page. You can grab it and install it if you'd like. However, doing it this way finishes the process for the users. They will be asked if they want to download the ActiveX helper. This means a gray dialog box pops up that often scares people, but there's no getting around it.

If you're interested, Microsoft also offers a "Font Smoother" at `http://www.microsoft.com/typography/grayscal/smoother.htm`. It helps to make your fonts look...well...smoother.

Using the Fonts

Okay, you've got the fonts downloaded into the cache. Now you need to incorporate them into the page. This is the easy part. At this point in time, the fonts act like they were already on the system to begin with because in reality, now they are on the system.

Follow these basic `FONT` and Style Sheet formats you've seen a million times before:

```
<FONT FACE="Amelia BT">Text Text</FONT>
<STYLE TYPE="text/css">
P {font-family: "AmeriGarmnd BT";}
</STYLE>
```

No matter how you incorporated fonts before, you can now use these to get up and running. Just do yourself a favor when you choose a font from a download site. Make a point of looking at the sample code. It often differs slightly. Notice from the preceding code the "`BT`" that is in the command? That isn't in the download name. Pay attention to things like that.

That's the basic concept. Finding the font you like might very well be the hardest part of all this dynamic font stuff. Good luck with it.

No Borders!

Here's the deal:

Netscape Navigator is a little late to the no margins party. Version 4.0 and above grasps the concept of three margin commands when entered into the `BODY` flag: `marginheight`, `marginwidth`, and the `overriding spacing`.

MSIE 3.0 is the starting point for margin manipulation for the Microsoft browser. A myriad of methods exist for killing margins there. In addition to grasping the three commands

Navigator uses, noted previously, Internet Explorer also offers five Style Sheet commands, one for each of the four sides and one for the total margin picture: `margin-left`, `margin-right`, `margin-top`, `margin-bottom`, and simply `margin` for all four sides.

In addition to the preceding format, MSIE also allows the use of frames to create a margin-less page.

Is it just me, or is the command `margin-bottom` just silly?

As with most fun things on the Web today, it takes two sets of commands to get the same effect on both browsers. But fear not, as also with things on the Web today, both sets of commands fit nicely on the same page and don't bump into one another. The commands not understood by the browser are simply ignored, and those the browser does understand are put into action.

 You can find this tutorial, and all of its examples, online at `http://www.htmlgoodies.com/ tutors/nomargins.html`.

 You can download just the examples at `http://www.htmlgoodies.com/wpg/`.

No Margins—Navigator

You know, I keep saying "no margins" because that's what prompted this tutorial, but in reality you can use these commands to create huge margins by setting the commands to huge numbers. You have control! Ah! The power! The power!

The concept here is as simple as it gets. Use one of three attributes, or just the spacing attribute, inside the document's `BODY` flag to set the margins, like so:

```
<body bgcolor="#ffffff" marginheight="0" marginwidth="0">
```

or

```
<BODY BGCOLOR="#ffffff" spacing="0">
```

Would you like to see it in action? Figure 4.1 shows the commands butting text and a big square image up against the side of the browser.

Obviously, using all four commands gives you greater control over each element in the browser window. Play with them; they're free. See what they do.

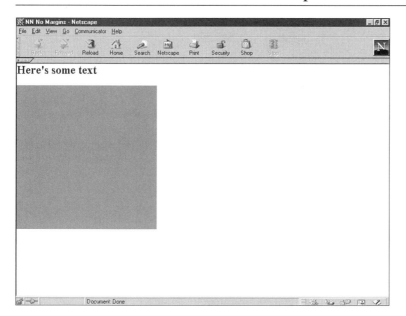

Figure 4.1
Pushed right up against the side.

No Margins—IE

If you say that heading out loud and real fast, it sounds as if you're in Texas and really happy about learning this.

OK! That's enough comedy! Let's get to it.

At this point, you're actually done because what I've shown you works in both browsers. But, as I've been told many times before, it wouldn't be an HTML Goodies tutorial if I didn't beat a point into the ground—literally.

In order to assure no borders across browsers, I use both the Netscape commands I showed previously and Style Sheet commands to affect IE. Again, if you want control of each of the sides, you can use these four:

```
margin-left

margin-right

margin-top

margin-bottom
```

You can specify margin widths in points (pt), inches (in), centimeters (cm), or pixels (px). Here's a quick example of each:

```
BODY {margin-left: 2pt}

BODY {margin-right: 12in}
```

```
BODY {margin-top: 45cm}

BODY {margin-bottom: 12px}
```

If you want to set any of the items to nothing, no indication of points, inches, pixels, or centimeters is needed. Just a zero will do.

Last, but not least, if you want to kill all margins, use the command margin. Here's a style block set to kill all margins around all sides of the IE browser window:

```
<HEAD>
<STYLE TYPE="text/css">
<!--
BODY {margin: 0}
-->
</STYLE>
</HEAD>
```

Figure 4.2 shows it in action. Make sure that you're using an IE browser, please. Well, at least make sure that what you're looking at is in an IE browser. I mean, this is a book after all.

Figure 4.2
Pushed right up against the side...again.

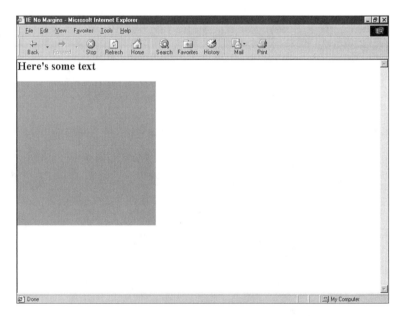

Do It with Frames

I offer this method first because it works, but in all honesty it's a bit of overkill. The commands already noted work just fine. There's no need to use anything else, but just remember that "beat an idea into the ground" statement earlier in this brilliant piece of tutorial. (If you think this is bad, you should hear me in class.)

In this instance, we'll set up a frameset with two frame windows. One will be set to zero, and the other will be set to 100%. The concept is to allow the commands within the framesets to set the margin gutter to zero. Here's the code:

```
<FRAMESET COLS="0,100%" BORDER="0" FRAMESPACING="0"
➥MARGINHEIGHT="0" MARGINWIDTH="0">
<FRAME SRC="invis.html" BORDER="0" FRAMESPACING="0"
➥MARGINHEIGHT="0" MARGINWIDTH="0">
<FRAME SRC="noborderright.html" BORDER="0" FRAMESPACING="0"
➥MARGINHEIGHT="0" MARGINWIDTH="0">
</FRAMESET>
```

The frameset is in columns with all elements set to zero. Ditto each element in each of the two frame SRCs. The result is shown in Figure 4.3.

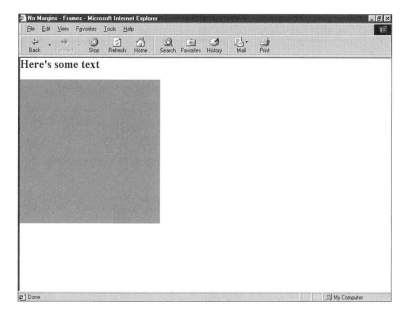

Figure 4.3
Yes, there's a frame there. It's just hidden.

Now, if you're using an MSIE browser, you got the correct effect. Those of you with Navigator probably didn't get the items butting right up against the left side. That's another downfall of this method; it's an IE-only deal in this format.

Yes, you can get Navigator to work with this format, but you need to put the commands previously discussed on the page that appears in the 100% frame window. If you do that, there's no need for the frames anyway. Just go with the border commands on a single page *sans* frames.

I actually like a little gutter around each side of my browser window. I think the background butting right up to the side is enough to pull it all together—but to each their own. If this is the effect you're looking for, now you have the tools to get the look across browsers.

Post by Screen Size

At the very heart of this tutorial is the ability to grab and display, or work with, the height and width of a user's screen. Figure 4.4 shows the first usage of this tutorial's coding.

Figure 4.4
This is a book, yes. You'll have to take my word for it.

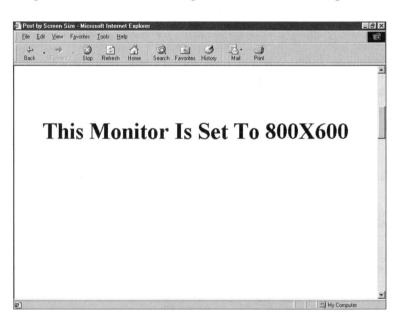

 You can find this tutorial, and all of its examples, online at http://www.htmlgoodies.com/ beyond/post_by_screen.html.

 You can download just the examples at http://www.htmlgoodies.com/wpg/.

I posted that info with a simple little JavaScript. It looks like this:

```
<SCRIPT LANGUAGE="javascript">
var width = screen.width
```

```
var height = screen.height
document.write("<B>You're set to "+width+ "X" +height+"</B>")
</SCRIPT>
```

Cool, huh? But knowing this information goes well beyond simply making paranoid people think that you're watching them through their computer screens. If you know the size of the person's monitor, you can use that information to your advantage.

I get letters all the time asking me how to make pages look good on all sized computer screens. I've offered some tips in the past, but it has still been a problem.

In this tutorial, I'm going to offer two scripts. One acts as a general, overall direction script. The user will be sent to a page designed for his screen. The second one is an internal script that writes items to the page depending on the user's screen settings. Let's start with the big one.

Redirection Choice

This little script works just like the traditional Browser Choice script. The script sits on a page by itself. The user logs in to the page and, depending on his screen settings, the user is sent to a specific page made for his screen settings.

The script only checks the user's monitor width settings to make the choice. Because scrolling is common on the Net, I don't see a need to check the height of the page.

The JavaScript code that returns the user's screen settings width is screen.width. So, using that info, we come up with the script that redirects the user. Remember, this script will probably never be seen by the user. You point your readers at a page that contains this script simply to get the redirecting effect. Thus, there is no need for images, extra text, or a lot of other fancy things.

You should, however, put Meta commands to the page if you intend to submit it to search engines.

Figure 4.5 shows the effect after the screen has run on a monitor set to 800X600.

Here's the script in its entirety:

```
<SCRIPT LANGUAGE="javascript">

if (screen.width == 1600)
{parent.location.href='1600page.html'}

if (screen.width == 1280)
{parent.location.href='1280page.html'}
```

```
if (screen.width == 1152)
{parent.location.href='1152page.html'}

if (screen.width == 1024)
{parent.location.href='1024page.html'}

if (screen.width == 800)
{parent.location.href='800page.html'}

if (screen.width == 640)
{parent.location.href='640page.html'}

if (screen.width <= 639)
{parent.location.href='text.html'}

</SCRIPT>
```

Figure 4.5
*A different page would
have displayed had my
user's screen setting been
different.*

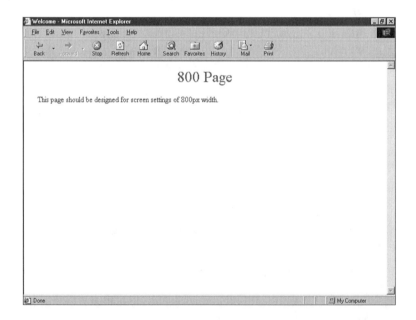

Remember, you won't see the script. It will simply take you to a new page created for your own screen setting.

The script is set to test for the most common screen width settings: 1600, 1280, 1152, 1024, 800, 640, and those below 640. I talked to a few of my computer friends, and they informed me that the chances you'll run into a screen width setting that differs from this is, quote, "small, if there at all."

Let me give you the basic concept of the script:

```
if (screen.width == 1600)
{parent.location.href='1600page.html'}
```

The script is set up as a series of IF statements. The browser checks one after the other down the line until the settings match. Notice the double equal sign. That's JavaScript for "is equal to."

After equality is found, the line of code within the curly brackets is triggered. In all cases, that code created a link in the parent window (the top level window), and the hypertext link was enacted. The script is written so that at least one of the IF statements will be true.

Internal Page Choice

Okay, the page redirection is usually enough to solve the situation, but it also means that you have to create multiple pages. That's a bit of work, and for some things it might be overkill.

Let's say that you have an image 850 pixels wide. For 800, 640, and below screen settings, that banner rolls off the screen and creates a horizontal scrollbar. This is not good. The easiest way to solve the problem is to create a 750px and a 630px version of the image for 800 and 640px browsers. All you need is a script that reads the browser width settings and writes the image code to the page so the correct image is posted. I happen to have such a script.

See the Script

This script works on much the same format as the script we just played with, but I make a couple more assumptions. You'll notice the same general IF statement set up:

```
if (screen.width < 639)
{document.write("Hello there")}
if (screen.width == 640)
{document.write("<IMG SRC=630px.gif>")}
if (screen.width == 800)
{document.write("<IMG SRC=750px.gif>")}
if (screen.width >= 1024)
{document.write("<IMG SRC=850px.gif>")}
```

It starts with the monitor tests. If the monitor setting is less than 639, the text "Hello there" is posted. After that, each screen size has an image posted. The image is different for each screen size so that it perfectly fits. Figure 4.6 is the result of using this script in a screen setting of 800X600. Note that the 750 pixel wide image is displayed.

Figure 4.6
Just right for 800X600.

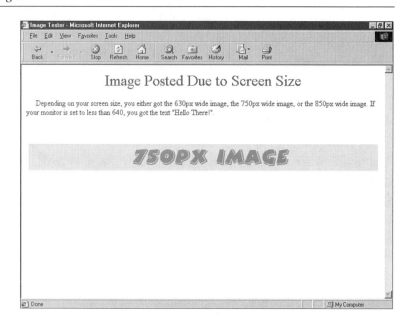

Next, the text looks for 640, 800, and anything 1024 and above. Note the >=. That means "greater than or equal to." If you want, you can continue the "equal to" format for all the screen sizes and create images for them all. I just figured that when the screen was wide enough—why keep making images?

Finally, notice that I get the image flag text to the page using a `document.write` statement. `document.write` does what it says. It writes text to the page. In this case, it writes the flag for a specific image to the page. Just remember, have any text you want written to the page in double quotes so that the JavaScript understands it is a text string and not a command to be followed.

The real beauty of this kind of scripting is that you only need one page. On that page is a script that posts differing items because of conditions. It's a very clever deal. In fact, I feel it's so clever that I have a tutorial on just this topic right here.

What more can I say? You've got the tools now to make sure that your pages fit the user's screen settings. Use it to make better, and better displaying, pages.

Internal Browser Test

This is really a clever deal. In this tutorial, I'm going to talk about a different way to post information to your page depending on what browser the user is running.

You can find this tutorial, and all of its examples, online at http://www.htmlgoodies.com/beyond/intbrowtest.html.

 You can download just the examples at http://www.htmlgoodies.com/wpg/.

It used to be that the favored method of posting elements that dealt with specific browsers was to use a browser choice script. Then, that script would send people to a whole separate page created just for their browsers. But that meant making a bunch of different pages. Here, I'm going to show you a method of putting that browser choice right on your page. A JavaScript will read the user's browser and, depending on what that person is running, post text and code to the page.

Now it will be possible to have both DHTML and Layer commands on the same page. Depending on whether the user is running IE or Navigator, he'll get the correct code for his system.

Just as we did in the screen size tutorial prior to this one, the very basic script format will allow us to grab and display information about the browser. Figure 4.7 is the concept in a very simple script.

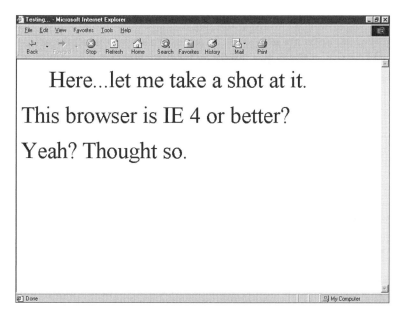

Figure 4.7
Another browser would have returned a different line of text.

How'd You Do That?

I did it through a JavaScript that first tests your browser's make and then tests your browser's version. Depending on the browser version and make, I posted the text "This browser is XXXX.x or better?". I just stuck the text "Here, let me take a shot at it" in front so that the JavaScript text would make a sentence. The text that follows is just straight text on the page.

But this is using the script in its easiest form. You can do so much more than a simple parlor trick, but first let's find out how I got the text to display correctly.

The Script

I'll show it to you in a second. First, let me tell you the thinking behind it.

There are so many different browsers and versions of browsers that to test for them all individually would be silly. You would do nothing but constantly update your scripts every time a new version comes out. So you need to make some broad, general statements. Here's what I test for in this script:

Is the browser Netscape Navigator, IE, or neither?

Is the browser version at least 4.0?

I made the second condition because it seems to be that browser version 4.0 was the turning point for both Netscape Navigator and Internet Explorer. Version 4.0 is when layers came to Netscape and when DHTML came to IE. That seems like a solid cutoff point because you can safely assume that all versions above 4.0 will continue to support what 4.0 does. Remember I'm giving you just the basic format here first.

That's enough description!

Here's the script that did the trick:

```
<SCRIPT LANGUAGE="javascript">

if (navigator.appName == "Microsoft Internet Explorer"
➥&& navigator.appVersion >= "4.0")
{document.write("This browser is IE 4 or better?")}

if (navigator.appName == "Microsoft Internet Explorer"
➥&& navigator.appVersion < "4.0")
{document.write("This browser is IE 3.x or less?")}

if (navigator.appName == "Netscape" && navigator.appVersion >= "4.0")
{document.write("This browser is Netscape 4 or better?")}
```

```
if (navigator.appName == "Netscape" && navigator.appVersion < "4.0")
{document.write("This browser is Netscape 3.x or less?")}

if (navigator.appName != "Microsoft Internet Explorer"
➥&& navigator.appName != "Netscape")
{document.write("This browser is not running IE or Netscape?")}

</SCRIPT>
```

Deconstructing the Script

I'll hit this step by step. After the first little blurb of code, you'll pretty much be able to take it the rest of the way, but here we go:

```
if (navigator.appName == "Microsoft Internet Explorer"
➥&& navigator.appVersion >= "4.0")
{document.write("Running IE 4 or better?")}
```

The script is a series of IF statements that tests the browser name and version. Read along in the previous code as I follow it through its test.

- if starts the command. The code that follows in the parentheses sets the test.
- navigator.appName is JavaScript for the name of the browser.
- Those double equal signs (==) mean "is equal to."
- The two names are "Netscape" and "Microsoft Internet Explorer." Notice the capitalization and double quotes. You have to have it just like this.
- The "&&" is JavaScript for "and." Thus, we're testing two elements here—the name of the browser and then what follows.
- navigator.appVersion is JavaScript for the browser's version number. Now, we'll get into this a little more later in the tutorial, but version numbers get tricky. However, as long as you denote the version in the "#.#" format and in double quotes as I have previously, you can make very broad statements such as, "Is the browser 4.0 or better?"
- >= means greater than or equal to. (<= means less than or equal to. You'll see that coming up.)
- "4.0" is my 4.0 cutoff point for version 4.0 browsers.

What follows within the curly brackets is what happens if the condition is met. In this case, a "document.write" statement is used to write text to the page. That's what document.write does. It simply writes what is within the double quotes to the page, no questions asked. Just make sure to have double quotes because without them, the script will think that the text refers to a command rather than simple text to be printed. Error!

In each of the following cases, I have text that denotes the browser version being printed to the page.

The next bit of code tests if the browser is IE and if it is less than version 4.0:

```
if (navigator.appName == "Microsoft Internet Explorer"
➥&& navigator.appVersion < "4.0")
{document.write("Running IE 3.x or less?")}
```

Next we test for Netscape browser and version 4.0 or better:

```
if (navigator.appName == "Netscape" && navigator.appVersion >= "4.0")
{document.write("Running Netscape 4 or better?")}
```

Here, we test for Navigator and versions less than 4.0:

```
if (navigator.appName == "Netscape" && navigator.appVersion < "4.0")
{document.write("Running Netscape 3.x or less?")}
```

Finally, we test to see if the user has neither Netscape nor Internet Explorer. "!=" means "is not equal to."

```
if (navigator.appName != "Microsoft Internet Explorer"
➥&& navigator.appName != "Netscape")
{document.write("not running IE or Netscape?")}
```

At least one of the conditions will be true and something will get written to the screen.

Notice that when I first had you look at the script, the first line of code (the "if" lines) was all on one line. Make sure that your code is like that. If not, you'll get an error.

A Better Example

Granted, this does take a little bit of coding to get through. But after you get the effect, you'll want to start using this stuff all over your pages to take advantage of what one browser will do that another won't—all while not leaving earlier version browsers out of the loop.

Okay, after that sentence, let me tell you what to look for in the next example:

- The script writes a link to HTML Goodies to the page.
- The script sets the same conditions as above.
- If the browser is IE version 4.0 or better, the link will take advantage of the IE 4.0 by setting the cursor to a question mark and popping up a ToolTip box.

If the browser is Netscape Navigator 4.0 or better, the layering function of that browser will come into play. When the mouse passes over, a purple box will pop up.

All other browsers get just a basic hypertext link.

Figure 4.8 shows the results in Internet Explorer 5.0.

Figure 4.8
Note the cursor and ToolTip box popping up.

Here's the Code

All I did was use very long document.write statements to write layer and/or SPAN flags and code to the page when a browser version 4.0 or better pops up. I know it looks confusing, but it's all pretty straightforward. Just go slow, and you'll get it. And once you do get one working, you'll go nuts with this stuff.

In order to save you a few headaches, here are some tips I learned the hard way when working with document.write statements:

- Any coding within document.write statements cannot contain double quotes, apostrophes, or commas unless an escape character is used. You'll find a tutorial on escape characters in Chapter 1, "Neat Stuff with Text."

- If you have a single word attribute (like BGCOLOR=white), there's no need to surround the items (white) with any quotes.

- Multiple word attributes (TITLE=Hey there) must be surrounded in single quotes:
  TITLE='Hey there'.

- ● `document.write` statements must all remain on the same line. Long lines are fine. Just don't break individual `document.write` lines into multiple lines.

- ● Try to avoid breaking code into multiple `document.write` statements, or you will get much error!

Getting Specific

You start to open a big can of worms, but sometimes it's needed. While writing this tutorial, I ran into a lot of trouble trying to separate out IE version 5.0. I figured that I could simply set up a statement that read that if the version is greater than or equal to 5.0, then do this. Makes sense, right?

Wrong.

You already know that `navigator.appName` represents the browser's name, and `navigator.appVersion` represents the browser's version. I know what each browser's name and version are because I first created a small JavaScript to return them to me. It looks like this:

```
<SCRIPT LANGUAGE="javascript">
document.write(navigator.appName)
document.write("<P>")
document.write(navigator.appVersion)
</SCRIPT>
```

Take that, paste it to a page, and run the script. You'll get the returns. You'll also notice that the version number is much bigger than what I'm showing you here.

I'm displaying the number simply by running part of the script I just gave you. See how much information there is? If you want to call for a specific browser, you're going to have to call for a specific version with that entire version code.

What a pain it is! Do you realize how many versions there are? Ugh! Wicked lots!

The IE 5.0 Problem

I figured this didn't really matter because each successive version would show itself by the first numbers, right? Make sense? Thus, IE 5.0 or better could be called by the number 5.0.

Wrong again.

Here's the version return from IE version 5.0:

```
4.0 (compatible; MSIE 5.0b2; Windows 95)
```

Nice, huh? It returns a 4.0 at the beginning. You must check this for every version above 5.0 that comes out after this book is published so that you can get them right.

Setting Your Page as Home Page: IE5.0 Only!

It is my suggestion to you that before you attempt to re-invent the wheel and create a script so huge that it includes all browsers and all versions, try this first.

For a specific browser and version, set up a script that will write text to the page if the browser and version are correct, but will write nothing if the condition is not met. Here's an example.

IE 5.0 will allow you to set up a link that, when clicked, will make your page the browser's home page. Annoying yes, but you can do it.

Here's the code I would use:

```
<SCRIPT LANGUAGE="javascript">
if (navigator.appName == "Microsoft Internet Explorer"
➥&& navigator.appVersion == "4.0 (compatible; MSIE 5.0b2; Windows 95)")
{
document.write("<STYLE><!--.homepage {behavior:url(#_IE_)}--></STYLE>")
document.write("<U><SPAN STYLE='color:blue;cursor:hand;' CLASS=homepage
ONCLICK='this.setHomePage(window.location);'> Make this your home page
➥</SPAN></U>")
}
else
{document.write("Make this page your Home Page!")}
</SCRIPT>
```

You have to have IE5.0 or better, or you'll just get text.

The concept is that if the exact condition is not met, the text is written to the page. If you want literally nothing written to the page, leave the document.write quotes empty. Those with the correct browser get the look; those without...don't.

I have seen multiple methods of doing this same effect. Most of the JavaScript I saw went into parsing and other commands. I wrote these scripts, so feel free to use them to your heart's content. I think they're functional and rather easy to understand. I hope you can use them.

No Selection Rectangle in IE

So, I'm at this conference, and I've just finished my presentation when a Goodies reader bops up and asks if there's any method of losing the dotted line that appears around the active links and active images in the Internet Explorer browser. I didn't know one off the top of my head, but I told him I'd certainly try to find out. This tutorial is my attempt to "certainly try to find out."

You'll find two methods here. The first allows the dots to pop up for just a moment (my favorite). The second loses the dots totally.

 You can find this tutorial, and all of its examples, online at `http://www.htmlgoodies.com/beyond/nodottedline.html`.

 You can download just the examples at `http://www.htmlgoodies.com/wpg/`.

The dotted line is technically called a "selection rectangle," and it was put there in order to help the user. The rectangle appears when the active text or image has focus brought to it. Or, to put it in layman's terms: when someone clicks on it. The rectangle remains as long as focus is on the element. In fact, the rectangle pretty much stays on the screen even if focus is moved from element to element through tabbing. It makes image maps look cruddy.

The thing is so persistent that it stays surrounding the active text or image even if the user clicks to go to another page and then returns using the Back button. You must be using Internet Explorer to see what I'm talking about! Dig Figure 4.9.

Figure 4.9
See the dotted box around the link just after I clicked on it?

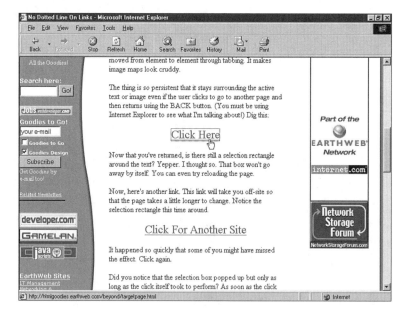

Figure 4.9 was created by clicking on the link and then immediately taking a screen capture. We went to the linked site and came back. Now that we've returned, is there still a selection rectangle around the text? Yuk! That box won't go away by itself. We even try reloading the page, but nothing happens.

First, some people like the selection rectangle but don't like it hanging around. They want it to pop up to denote the click and then go away. If that's you, here's the code to get that effect:

```
<A HREF="http://www.vhnd.com"
onClick="if(navigator.appName == 'Microsoft Internet Explorer')
➥this.blur()">
Click For Another Site</a>
```

The onClick is what does the trick. It's a little more than it needs to be because I have it set to test the browser and only react if it's Internet Explorer. All you really need is the this.blur() command, like so:

```
<A HREF="http://www.hairclub.com" onClick="this.blur()">
Click For Another Site</a>
```

The command is set up so that as soon as the click, the forced focus, is over, focus is taken off the element and the selection box goes away. The preceding onClick format can be copied and pasted into a hypertext link no matter whether the active area is text or an image. It works great for image maps.

Lose It Altogether

I actually like the selection rectangle popping up. I just don't want it to stay. I want it to appear and leave that fast. Some of you might not want it at all. For that, we need a little different coding.

Figure 4.10 is a link that has been clicked. Note it is a different color having been activated. There's no selection rectangle. One never popped up.

That's pretty cool, huh? Here's the code:

```
<a href=http://www.hairclub.com onFocus="if(this.blur)this.blur()">
Hair Club for Men</a>
```

Notice that once focus is brought to the element, the blur is stopped twice. It's a double blur! Use this, and you'll get no rectangle at all.

So, in response to that guy at the conference: I told you I'd find out.

Figure 4.10
Ah, no box.

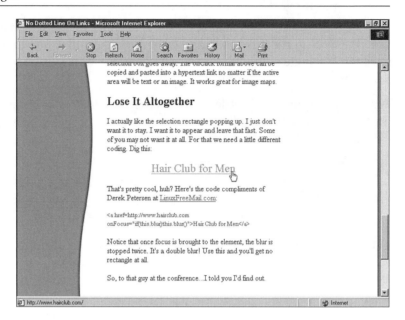

Resize Your Browser Window

Have you seen this effect yet? Some people like it, but others hate the tar out of it. Here's the concept:

You have a page that's designed for a 600X800 screen size. There are multiple methods to getting that effect to display correctly on monitors set higher or lower. You could encase your page in a table cell set to 600X800. That's called a fixed design. You could use JavaScript to grab the person's screen settings and display a page created for his screen settings. I have a tutorial on that earlier. You could also set up a frame format set to display the 600X800 format no matter what the user's screen settings.

Today, I'm seeing a new method. Forget setting your pages to fit the user's browser; set the user's browser to fit your pages.

 You can find this tutorial, and all of its examples, online at `http://www.htmlgoodies.com/ beyond/resizewindow.html.`

 You can download just the examples at `http://www.htmlgoodies.com/wpg/.`

The code to get the effect is so simple I never thought about putting up a tutorial. I just posted it to the discussion groups or sent it back through email. After I started sending out the code, the letters began coming back asking how to get the browser window to return to the user's previous setting after he left the page. Ah ha! I smelled a tutorial.

Resize the Window

Here's the code that resizes the window:

```
<SCRIPT>
window.resizeTo(600,800);
</SCRIPT>
```

Take that code and put it between the <HEAD> flags on your page. You want it up that high so that the browser resizes before the rest of the page loads.

You can probably tell from the numbers that the first deals with the X, or horizontal axis. The second deals with the Y, or vertical axis.

When you use the format, only the right and bottom sides of the browser window come in. The top and left remain stationary.

My personal reference books state that the resizeTo command works on Netscape Navigator browsers 4.0 and above. I also happen to know that the command works on Internet Explorer browsers 5.0. Because the command works only on some higher level browsers, you might want to use a browser detect script to send people using that browser to the page that contains the commands. All others should get a fixed design page.

OK! That's enough description! Let's get to the look-see. When you click this link, the browser screen resizes to 300X300. I went small so that all could see the effect.

Figure 4.11 show this tutorial's online version at full size. Figure 4.12 shows the same screen after I clicked on the link. You notice the browser resized. You'll also get to see my messy desktop.

Get It Back to Size

Let's fix that problem.

You might think that a user has to press the Back button for this resize script to fire. Nope! It's set to trigger using an onUnload Event Handler, so simply leaving the page gets the effect. How the user leaves doesn't matter.

Here's the script:

```
<SCRIPT LANGUAGE="javascript">
var width = screen.width
var height = screen.height
document.write("<BODY onUnload=window.resizeTo("+width+ ","
➧+height+")>")
</SCRIPT>
```

103

Figure 4.11
Okay, Houston. Everything looks normal. Preparing to click.

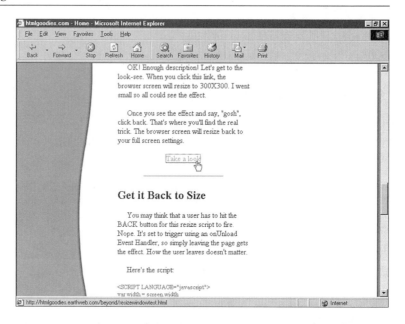

Figure 4.12
Uh, Houston, we might have a problem here.

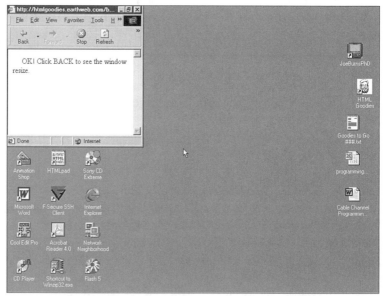

Placement of this script is important. This script will write the BODY flag to your page. See that in the document.write statement?

You'll have to close the BODY flag in the text of the HTML document by simply adding </BODY> at the end, just above the </HTML>. You know...where it always goes. The preceding script simply creates the begin BODY flag.

Here's the trick; the current screen height and screen width are grabbed when the page loads and sets to the variables width and height.

Those values are then used to build another resizeTo() command. That command sits in the BODY flag and when the user leaves the page, it resizes the browser back to full size.

If you have other statements inside your BODY flag, you need to make a point of putting them into the script as well.

In all honesty, pages that resize usually don't offer this effect. I'm sure the thinking is that the user can always click to full-size his browser.

Enjoy the resizeTo() command. It's a pretty nice thing to use to resize the browser to your pages. I just wonder how your user will feel about it.

Printable Pages

This is an extremely popular thing to have these days. Many of my favorite Web sites, including all the great sites owned by EarthWeb and Internet.com, are offering "printable" versions of their pages.

In the past, if you wanted to print a page, you simply printed the page. That meant also printing all the banner ads, other links, and maybe even the background. That just killed those expensive three-color cartridges. Now, in order to assist surfers who print, often you'll see a little printer icon that claims to send you to a more "printable" page. Usually that means just the text, maybe one banner ad, and a couple of links at the bottom.

I've been getting some letters lately asking what should be done in order to create a printable page, so I did some checking. Here are the results of that search.

 You can find this tutorial, and all of its examples, online at http://www.htmlgoodies.com/ *tutors/printpage.html.*

 You can download just the examples at http://www.htmlgoodies.com/wpg/.

What Do You Want to Print?

First, answer the big question. What do you want to print? I don't mean what text. I think we can all agree that it's the text of the page that you want to print. The question is, do you want just the text, or do you want other elements?

Often, sites put a banner ad at the top or the bottom of the printable page. That's up to you. My suggestion, and the results of my research into the subject, warns you away from offering anything but the text of the article. The thinking goes that I looked at your banner ads on the original page. You offered me a page to print. Please don't give me more than I asked for.

I would specifically avoid putting any format text like, "This page formatted to print in [browser]," "This page will print best in IE," or "Print this page in Landscape," or internal page links as well. In fact, avoid putting in any links! The user cannot use the links from a printed page.

The only element I would add to the printable page would be a reference cite, as you would find in the reference section of a research paper. I would even make a point of putting the cite first. Follow a basic format, one like you learned in your high school English class, so that someone who prints the page can easily cite you in a paper or article. Plus...by putting a cite on your page, you mark it as yours. That's a smart thing to do.

Other than that, think long and hard about putting anything other than the text of the page on a printable page.

How Do You Want It to Print?

When I began searching around for answers, this was the question most prominent in my mind. You see, many of the printable pages I have seen do not take format into account. For the most part, the printable page is just text, running all the way across the page. What prints actually doesn't render like it appears on the screen. Furthermore, if the user has an older printer, the paragraphs won't stay in nice tight compact groups. The lines will truncate, and you'll get that lovely long line, short line, long line, short line format.

Ick!

Let me suggest that if you offer a printable page, format the page to display, and thus print, in a format that can be easily transferred to a printer.

You would be amazed at how many different formats people proclaim will be successful when printing. There are any number of characters, lines, fonts, and elements per inch that you can get into. After going through them all, here are what I consider the parameters most likely to produce a successful print.

- No more than 65 characters (including spaces) per line.
- No more than 66 lines per page.

Yes, I saw the statements that one can get away with 70, or even 72, characters per line. I chose the preceding parameters because they came from the copy rules of a direct marketing firm. Their research found that we humans are most happy with 65 characters in 66 lines.

In addition, those numbers fall within the default print ranges of just about any printer from the expensive laser printer all the way down to the lowly 16-pin dot matrix.

These rules are taking into consideration that you are using a combination of upper- and lowercase letters and that the user has his browser set to the default settings. If you run into a person who has his text set to 24 point, you're kind of dead no matter what you do. The print is going to look crummy. The rules change somewhat if you write in all lowercase or all uppercase. In my word processing program, I was able to get 91 lowercase characters in the same space only 64 uppercase characters would fit. I used Times New Roman font, which is the overwhelming default font used today.

The one thing you never want to do is to offer a user just a simple text version of your page. I have seen printable pages that are little more than a copy and paste of the text saved in .txt format. That looks terrible and doesn't print well at all.

You will need to do some formatting.

Get That Format

In looking for methods of setting text to a specific width, I found a lot of tips and tricks that just do not work. For example:

> One site claimed that putting the style attribute `STYLE="width:50ex"` in the page's body command would set the number of letters across a page to 50, or whatever you set the number to be. It displays only in Netscape Navigator, and I mean it displays. Try printing it, and you'll have big problems.

> Another site proclaimed that you could force the page to print in Landscape by adding the command `<PAGESIZE ORIENTATION="landscape">`. You're a better person than I am if you can get it to work. I tried it all over the page, but no dice. There is a command similar to this in UNIX, but I couldn't get the effect.

"So what?" you ask.

I'm simply pointing out that most of the fancy coding or altering of the person's browser will not work. If you are going to offer a printable page, you need to play to the lowest common printer denominator. Don't offer a page that must print in Landscape. Redesign it so that the page will print in the more common profile format.

The best method I've found for creating a printable page is a simple table cell set to 400 pixels wide. The basic code of the page will look something like this:

```
<TABLE BORDER="0" WIDTH="400">
<TR><TD>
Text to be printed here
</TD></TR>
</TABLE>
```

The simplest coding is always the best and is always understood by the largest number of browsers. I can get the exact same effect by using Style Sheet commands, but why? This is much easier and more browser friendly.

A Color Rule

Yes, yes, I know that your page is olive green with fuchsia highlights over an off-yellow body of text that melds politely with a mauve glisten of lime tones. However...

Your printable page should probably be black text on a white background.

I think that about covers it.

Typography Concerns

When you create your printable page, you'll want to keep the major typography. By that I mean the headers, the paragraph structure, and any other text placement. For instance, if you have a list on the main page, you'll keep that list format on the printable page.

I do not think that text decoration should carry over unless it is absolutely required. Bold and underline are not big offenders. They will both print pretty well. It's the italic text you should avoid. It just doesn't print very well, especially on earlier model printers.

I don't want to go as far as to say to never use italic, but I'd like to come close. If you use italic on your Web page, go with quotes or underline on the printable page.

Watch also offering a page that has text set to a lower point setting than the default. If you have negative one or two font text on the main page, try to lose that on the printable page.

I would also try to keep all the text in the same font on the print page. It just gives a more uniform look.

Basically, the printable page should be uniform in format to the original page, yet it should be less ornate. Go bland. The user is printing because he wants the content, not the design. If he wanted the design, he would have printed the original page.

Right?

Images

When this tutorial first appeared online, I didn't say much about images on this printable page. My mind-set was to lose the images. However, a few people wrote in and asked about charts or graphs or even required images, so I did some more sleuthing around.

The basic concerns always come back to the printing. Here are some tips that I found:

- Go with black and white equals of your images if possible.

- Images that can be set to "line art" should be. Line art would be the image, saved as a GIF, at the two-color level. This would include graphs, charts, and other images simpler than a photograph.

- The background of the image should be white so that no lines appear around the edges.

- If color is required, use GIF format using as few colors as possible to allow the image to still look good. I suggest GIF because it immediately sets the level to no more than 256 colors. Remember, you do not know what level of printer the user has, so make it as easy on the printer as possible.

- Finally, attempt to set up the Web page so that the image remains on the same printed page as the description that goes with it.

This means that you'll have to learn to play with page breaks.

Page Breaks

Okay, here's a tricky one. I read a site that stated you should make a point of incorporating page breaks into your printable pages. As far as I can think, there are two basic methods of getting the page breaks. The first is to design your printable pages and then add "whitespace" where the page would naturally break.

You can get the effect by adding <BR> commands where the page would naturally break. Just keep checking your work in the Print Preview sections of Netscape and Internet Explorer. I tried it. You'll have to add a little extra space where the page breaks, but it's not that hard to get.

The second method is to use the Style Sheet page-break-after format. This is actually the lesser of the two choices in that it only works in Internet Explorer. Plus, it's difficult to set it to break at a certain point rather than just at a heading format. I have an entire tutorial on it right here.

So which do you use? Well, in all honesty, unless the page breaks really matter, neither. I don't know that page breaks are overly important. The only real concerns are if an important section is disrupted by a page break or if the page break format is crucial to the format (like a manuscript or book format).

If the page breaks are that important to the piece, maybe you'll want to offer the piece as a download to a word processing program or as an Adobe Acrobat PDF file format.

If you do decide to go with the page breaks and don't want the Word or Adobe format, I would suggest the creation of whitespace is your best bet.

If you are going to offer a printable page, understand that you are going to create more work for yourself. You'll not only have to create the original page, but also its printable equal. And…as your parents have told you one too many times, "If you are going to do something, do it right."

If you offer someone the ability to print your page, make it so that the page will print correctly over the largest number of browsers.

Following the suggestions I have laid out here, the printable version of this page would look like Figure 4.13. I tried setting whitespace for the page breaks. The entire process took me about seven minutes.

Figure 4.13
This creates a nicely printed page without a ton of additional images the user simply does not want.

Rounded Corners in Tables

One of the knocks against HTML is that it's blocky. Designs are too squared off. This is especially true of tables. They are always four sided with nice, sharp corners.

Lately though, I am seeing some great programming that basically uses those sharp cornered tables to create softened shapes. I asked a question one time in my HTML class here on campus. The question read, "It is possible to have tables with rounded corners...true or false."

The answer is false, but a lot of students missed it because they would swear that they had seen tables with rounded corners. I attempted to explain that the tables were quite square. What was inside the table cells gave the illusion of the rounded corners. Yes, it was a lousy test question and has since been retired.

 You can find this tutorial, and all of its examples, online at `http://www.htmlgoodies.com/tutors/roundcorners.html`*.*

 You can download just the examples at `http://www.htmlgoodies.com/wpg/`*.*

The process of getting rounded corners and other rounded shapes through tables is rather easy. In fact, I've now used the process a few times on some different Web sites. My latest use is on my University personal homepage. Take a look at Figure 4.14. Notice how the corners of the orange "card" are rounded. If you can't quite make it out from Figure 4.14, you'll find the actual site at `http://www.selu.edu/Academics/Faculty/jeburns/`.

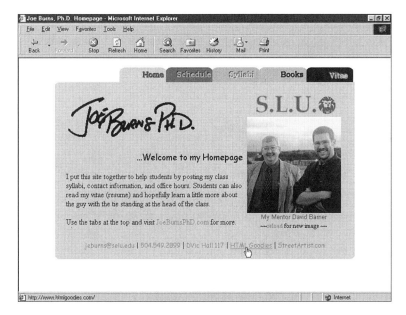

Figure 4.14
Note the rounded corners. It really softens the page and the effect of the note cards.

Here's another example I finished and posted on 7/27/01. Figure 4.15 has nothing to do with this tutorial beyond being another example of using tables to round corners. This one is a little more dramatic with longer, sweeping lines. It's a page for the Southeastern Louisiana University chapter of Phi Kappa Phi. You'll find it at `http://www.selu.edu/orgs/ PhiKappaPhi/`.

Figure 4.15
You have to be smart to be in this club, let me tell you!

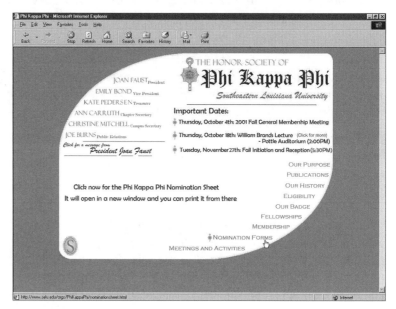

Those rounded corners were achieved through the use of tables and some small square images that give the impression that one corner has been rounded off. Let's take a look at how it's done.

The Table Structure

Here's the deal. In order to achieve this effect, you're going to have to understand tables and how they work. You will most likely have to know how to set a table cell's height and width, and possibly know how to use the COLSPAN and ROWSPAN commands as well. If any of that is Greek to you, see my original table tutorials online at HTMLGoodies.com before going on. I won't be getting into the basics of table creation here.

The table that created the "card" in Figure 4.14 is set up so that three "corners" are set aside. That way, I can fill that corner with a small image that has its corner rounded off. If that didn't make much sense, stay tuned. It'll get easier. Figure 4.16 is the same thing as Figure 4.15 except with the table walls exposed.

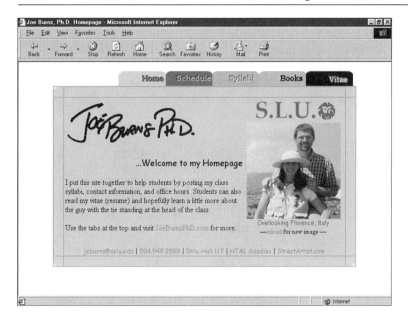

Now you can most likely see why you'll need to know the ins and outs of using height and width commands in your table cells. That table in Figure 4.16 has a height and a width set for every cell so that it retains its shape.

Once again—EVERY cell has both a height and a width. Don't rely on only putting one width per column or one height per row. Set them all to force the computer's hand.

The Corner Images

Figure 4.17 displays the three corner images that were used to create the effect. I have them in a table cell with the background set to black so that you can see the image's shape a little better.

Figure 4.17
They're small, but you can still see the rounded edges. You might even want to look at the previous screen captures to pick out which corner went where.

I named the images `orangeupperleft.gif`, `orangelowerleft.gif`, and `orangelowerright.gif` just so I could keep them straight as to where they went in the grand scheme.

They're Not All Images

If you look at the table format again, you'll notice large sections of orange. Because the little corners are images, you might think that the larger sections are also images. That's not the case. They are just table cells that have a BGCOLOR set that equals the corner image's color. Figure 4.18 has a red "X" on the table cells that get their color through a BGCOLOR command rather than an image.

Figure 4.18
It's almost all BGCOLOR.

It's basically everything other than the corner images themselves.

The thing you **must** keep in mind is that when creating the corner images, the color you use must be the exact same hex-code color as you will use in the table cell backgrounds. That way, the images and the cells with color will meet up flawlessly.

And speaking of making those images...

Making the Images

Before I get into the images, let me explain that this is how I do it. I am by no means saying that this is the only method to getting the effect. This is simply how I get the rounded corner.

My preferred image-editing program is Paint Shop Pro. I have the full version. You can try out a 30-day version of the program by visiting www.Jasc.com.

Now we move along to the good stuff. These are the steps I use to create the look:

1. Before you do any image work, lay out the page and build the table. Build it using height and width attributes in each of the table cells. Build it with the colors you want to use. Choose a background color for the page. Note that the background of the page in Figure 4.14 is white; thus the "rounding" effect is achieved by making part of what will be a square image white.

   I would suggest that you try to get your corner images square. It will make things a whole lot easier later on.

Are you still with me? Everything is square. You are simply giving the illusion of roundness by taking a square image and rounding a corner. If that image has the same color as the background and the same color as the remainder of the table, the effect will blend in perfectly.

I say to do all of that first because by first building the table and choosing the colors, you will know exactly how large an image you will require and what color you will use to create the image. In addition, you'll know what color to use to blend the corner of the image into the background.

Now that you have all that, move along.

2. Now let's build the corner pieces. Let's say that your corner pieces are going to be 100X100. Note again that the image is square.

   In your image editor, create an image that is 100X100 filled with the same color as the background as the page. Now you know it will blend into the background.

   Now choose to use your image editor's Shape tool. This is the tool that will allow you to draw a shape on the 100X100 image. You should be able to choose from many different shapes. You want to choose to draw a circular shape. Make sure that the Shape tool will only draw the shape. Do not allow the tool to fill in the shape it draws.

> ### Note
>
> You want to draw your circle so that the arc meets the edges of the image at the same number of pixels along the top edge as along the side edge. If that doesn't happen, you get a lopsided arc. Maybe you want that look. If so, go for it. I'm just staying basic for this tutorial. Later on, you can try all kinds of strange and wonderful arc formats.
>
> To get the effect, find the exact middle of your image. This is why a perfectly square image is best to work with. The exact middle will be half the length and half the width. So, the exact middle of our 100X100 image is the 50, 50 pixel point. Most image editors will show you the pixels points as you roll your pointer over the image.
>
> Get your pointer to that exact middle point and click. As you start to drag your mouse, the circle will begin to draw. Keep dragging until the circle touches all four sides at the same time. When it happens, unclick. You should get something that looks like Figure 4.19.

3. This is the basis for all of your arcs. Notice how you now have a square image broken into five sections. This single image can now act as any corner. In fact, it can act as both an internal or external corner. All you need to do now is use your image editor's Fill function to fill in the color. The Fill function is usually denoted by a little paint can tipping a drop of paint.

115

Figure 4.19
A circle touching all four sides of the square it is sitting in. To get the effect, you must have your circle touch all four sides.

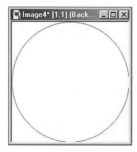

Just make sure to fill in the correct parts to create the correct corner. Figure 4.20 is an upper left-hand corner.

Figure 4.20
Just fill in the parts until the only thing left is the empty arc.

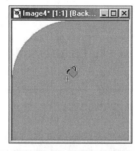

Tip

More than likely, your corners will all be the same size. If they're not, redo the table and get them all the same size. Once you have the square with the circle drawn, save it. Now you have a single image that will create every corner. The corners will look more uniform that way.

Simply open the circled image, fill in what you want and then choose Save As to save the image under a new name. Re-open the round image again and fill in for the next corner. Just keep doing that, and you'll have four uniform corners.

4. Internal corners will use the exact same format. You'll just fill in different sections of the image and erase what's left of the circle. Figure 4.21 is an upper left internal corner.

I erase the unwanted circle lines by choosing the image program's Shapes tool, setting it to the background color, and also setting it to fill in the color rather than just draw the shape. I then chip away at the lines.

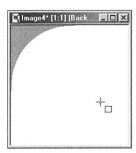

Now you've got the images. Just plug them in to the table you've already built, and you should get nice rounded corners inside of a square table.

Here's one more hint. When building the table, set the border to zero and make a point of running all the table code together. Do not leave any spaces from <TABLE> to </TABLE>, and the cells will butt right up against each other.

Fullscreen Effect

More screen Scotty! I need more screen!

Perform this text in a stunning Captain Kirk voice. It'll really sound cool. Trust me.

This is one of those tricks that people either love or they hate. Fullscreen mode is the ability to open the browser screen to the full monitor size. It is available in both Internet Explorer and Netscape Navigator. The main difference is the Title bar. You get one with Netscape Navigator, but you don't with Internet Explorer.

Some say that it's great for display. I agree to a point. The main concern I have is that it's lousy for navigation. To that end, I wouldn't suggest creating an entire site that functions in the full screen unless you provide your own Back and Forward buttons. Without them, the surfer is kind of lost. Not everyone knows to right-click and use the navigation there.

Okay then, let's do it.

 You can find this tutorial, and all of its examples, online at `http://www.htmlgoodies.com/beyond/fullscreen.html`.

 You can download just the examples at `http://www.htmlgoodies.com/wpg/`.

Open in Fullscreen Mode

You can get to fullscreen mode two ways. You can have the window simply open full screen by itself or set up a button or link that will open the window.

Internet Explorer users can also get to a kind-of fullscreen mode by just pressing F11. If you're using MSIE, try it. Press F11 again to return to normal mode. Because it doesn't work in Netscape Navigator, I am not making it a subheading. I just wanted to mention it so you'll know the trick.

Let's start with just opening the browser in fullscreen mode. It's easy. Copy and paste this into the page's HEAD flag section:

```
<script>
window.open("bigpage.html","fs","fullscreen,scrollbars")
</script>
```

That format will give you scrollbars. If you don't want scrollbars, just alter the code a bit to this:

```
<script>
window.open("bigpage.html","fs","fullscreen=yes")
</script>
```

Note that the `"fs"` is simply a name I assigned to the page. You really don't even need that in there. The page will open without it. But what if you want to give the users the ability to close the window? Well then...

Close It Up

You might take it from the preceding italic statements that the newly opened full screen can be closed through pressing F11. Nope! You need to offer the user the ability to close the window. Add this code to the newly opened page:

```
<A HREF="#" OnClick="window.close('fs')">Close window</A>
```

That will offer a link that closes the window named "fs". See why I used a name for the page?

If you'd like a button that closes the window, try this:

```
<FORM>
<INPUT TYPE="button" VALUE="Close the Window"
➥onClick="window.close('fs')">
</FORM>
```

Click to Fullscreen Mode

This is how I see the fullscreen mode used most often: A button or link is made available that opens a new window in full screen.

Here's the code for the button and the script:

```
<script>
<!--
function fullwin(){
window.open("bigpage.html","bfs","fullscreen,scrollbars")
}
//-->
</script>
<center>
<form>
<input type="button" onClick="fullwin()"
➥value="Open Full Screen Window">
</form>
</CENTER>
```

It's just a basic button that triggers the function equal to what I showed you earlier to open a window on-the-fly. You can paste the function in the HEAD section of the document and the button to the body if you'd like. I don't. I just plop it all in where I want the button.

Now you know the trick. It's a very blatant effect that really pops up and out of nowhere. Use it wisely. Use it when it helps the user. Don't just use it because you like it. Make sure that you have a viable reason to use the effect.

Figure 4.22 displays how big the full screen will be.

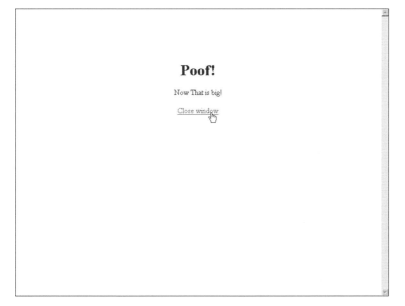

Figure 4.22
Whoa! That's big!

119

Pop-Under Windows

When something new hits the Web, whether it's good or bad, the email pours into HTML Goodies asking how to get the effect. Most of the time, the resulting tutorial makes a lot of people happy. This one might not.

Many of you might be familiar with pop-up ads. Well, the latest incarnation of those ads are what are called "pop-under" ads. These are basic JavaScript driven new windows that pop up behind the main window rather than lying over the top.

Advertisers love them because they are new and are causing a stir. Surfers are less enthusiastic. To that end, I'll probably take some heat for posting this tutorial, but my job is only to give code and not judge how one uses it.

Like how I danced around that one?

The Basic Thinking

Okay, here's the thinking. In order for a new window to fall behind the parent window, we're going to have to do what's known as blurring focus on that new window. You might have noticed in your own surfing that pop-under windows do quickly show up as an outline and then fall back behind the main window. That quick appearance is the new window coming to full focus. After that focus is on the window, commands in the code immediately blur that window's focus and it falls behind.

In order to assign that blur to the entire window, we will have to assign that window a single JavaScript variable name. That way, whatever effect we put to that variable name affects the entire window. Get it? Okay, let's look at the code:

```
<SCRIPT LANGUAGE="JavaScript">
function goNewWin() {
//***Get what is below onto one line***
TheNewWin =window.open("popunderexample.html",'TheNewpop','toolbar=1,
location=1,directories=1,status=1,menubar=1,
scrollbars=1,resizable=1');
//***Get what is above onto one line***
TheNewWin.blur();
}
</SCRIPT>
<CENTER>
<FORM>
```

```
<input type="button" VALUE="click me!" onClick="goNewWin()">
</FORM>
</CENTER>
```

The code is pretty straightforward. First, we set a function I titled "`goNewWin()`". That function allows us to call on the entire effect when we want to.

Next you'll notice that the basic `window.open` pop-up window format is assigned to the variable `TheNewWin`. That is so we can now affect the entire new window by simply attaching the effect to a single variable.

Please note the lines in the code that suggest you get that entire new window text on one line. That's rather important if you're not a big fan of JavaScript errors. Finally, we get to the line that makes the magic:

```
TheNewWin.blur();
```

Just as I said before, we attach the `blur()` effect to the variable name representing the entire new window. Please keep the empty parentheses after the blur command. You have to have those.

I finished up the example by setting the function to fire using a basic form button:

```
<CENTER>
<FORM>
<input type="button" VALUE="click me!" onClick="goNewWin()">
</FORM>
</CENTER>
```

More than likely, you won't use the effect this way. I am just doing it to show you the effect on command. In fact, let's see the effect...on command.

The Effect

This one's a little hard to show, so what I did was make my browser window smaller than full screen and popped up a new window. Figure 4.23 shows both windows. Notice the new window is behind the main parent window that spawned it.

121

Figure 4.23
*Here window, window,
window. Don't be shy.*

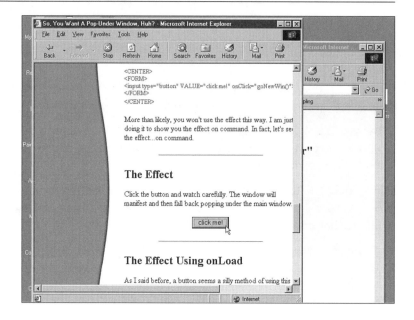

The Effect Using *onLoad*

As I said before, a button seems to be a silly method of using this format. You want the effect to fire as soon as the page loads. In order to get that, you'll simply delete the preceding HTML button code and fire the function using the onLoad Event Handler in the BODY flag. It'll look something like this:

```
<BODY BGCOLOR="FFFFFF" onLoad="goNewWin()">
```

Now you have the code for popping under all the windows you desire. Just keep in mind that surfers aren't exactly thrilled with new pop-up windows. They might not be overly giddy about new pop-under windows. Use this only when needed, and try not to use it to force a surfer's hand.

New Window: No Title Bar

In my tutorial dedicated to opening new windows through JavaScript, I made the statement that you could not open a new window that didn't have a title bar. Don't check. It doesn't say that any more.

A reader saw that statement, informed me that he knew of a method, and gave me the basics. I took those steps and put together the script in this tutorial. It's a new window that opens without a title bar. The effect is created by using the open.window JavaScript, along with the fullscreen code discussed in this tutorial.

Sorry to say that even though the fullscreen and JavaScript commands work in Netscape, the loss-of-title-bar effect only works in Internet Explorer. However, I've bulked up the script so that not only do you have control over the title bar, but also over the window's size and placement on the screen. It's a neat little piece of work. Dig Figure 4.24.

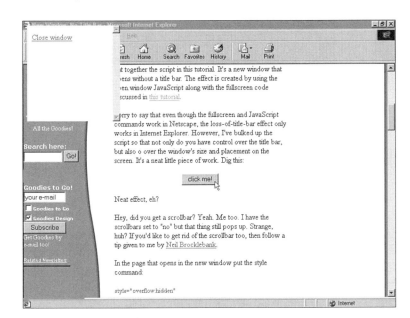

Figure 4.24
Neat window! Keep reading, and I'll tell you how to lose that scrollbar.

Neat effect, eh?

Hey, did you get a scrollbar? Yeah. Me too. I have the scrollbars set to "no," but that thing still pops up. Strange, huh? If you'd like to get rid of the scrollbar too, follow a tip given to me by Neil Brocklebank.

In the page that opens in the new window, put the following `style` command

```
style="overflow:hidden"
```

in the BODY flag. Now, remember! That goes in the BODY flag of the page that is opening inside the new window, not the page that contains the script. That's real important.

The Button Code

It goes like this:

```
<CENTER>
<FORM>
<input type="button" VALUE="click me!" onClick="goNewWin()">
```

```
</FORM>
</CENTER>
```

It's a basic FORM button that is set up to fire a function named "goNewWin()". That's about all there is to it. Let's see that script.

The Script Code

The script is inside of a function. Here it is:

```
<script language="JavaScript">
function goNewWin() {
// Set height and width
var NewWinHeight=200;
var NewWinWidth=200;
// Place the window
var NewWinPutX=10;
var NewWinPutY=10;
//Get what is below onto one line
TheNewWin =window.open("untitled.html",'TheNewpop',
'fullscreen=yes,toolbar=no,location=no,directories=no,
status=no,menubar=no,scrollbars=no,resizable=no');
//Get what is above onto one line
TheNewWin.resizeTo(NewWinHeight,NewWinWidth);
TheNewWin.moveTo(NewWinPutX,NewWinPutY);
}
</script>
```

We start by setting four parameters:

```
// Set height and width
var NewWinHeight=200;
var NewWinWidth=200;
// Place the window
var NewWinPutX=10;
var NewWinPutY=10;
```

Right now, I have the height and width of the new window set to 200. I have the position of the window set to 10 pixels down from the top and 10 pixels in from the left. Keep the basic format, but feel free to set the numbers to whatever positions and parameters you'd like.

124

Next, we set the open window code to the variable, "TheNewWin". By doing that, we can then manipulate the window by manipulating the variable name:

```
//Get what is below onto one line
TheNewWin =window.open("untitled.html",'TheNewpop',
'fullscreen=yes,toolbar=no,location=no,directories=no,
status=no,menubar=no,scrollbars=no,resizable=no');
//Get what is above onto one line
```

See the two comments that suggest all of that should be on one line? Pay attention to that. If you're getting errors with this script, I'll bet dollars to donuts that's your problem.

Notice you can set all the parameters just like any other new window code. Notice also that the fullscreen parameter is now stuck in there. That's what does the no-title bar trick.

Now let's play with the parameters you set at the top of the script:

```
TheNewWin.resizeTo(NewWinHeight,NewWinWidth);
TheNewWin.moveTo(NewWinPutX,NewWinPutY);
```

See how the variables of the height and width, top and left, are brought into play affecting TheNewWin? That's how to apply the parameters to the new window.

That's very cool.

OnLoad *the Window*

I have the script set up to fire when a button is clicked. I get that by putting the script into a function format. If you'd like the script to fire as soon as the page loads, you'll need to get it out of the function format and place it into the HEAD section of the page. The script looks like this:

```
<script language="JavaScript">
// Set height and width
var NewWinHeight=200;
var NewWinWidth=200;
// Place the window
var NewWinPutX=10;
var NewWinPutY=10;
//Get what is below onto one line
TheNewWin =window.open("untitled.html",'TheNewpop',
'fullscreen=yes,toolbar=no,location=no,directories=no,
status=no,menubar=no,scrollbars=no,resizable=no');
//Get what is above onto one line
TheNewWin.resizeTo(NewWinHeight,NewWinWidth);
```

```
TheNewWin.moveTo(NewWinPutX,NewWinPutY);
</script>
```

Notice it's just the same script without the function code and button. This way, the script will fire when it's loaded into RAM.

Part II

Playing Around with Forms

Chapter 5

Good Looking Forms

One area of Web design that people often overlook is how their forms are created. Most think it is acceptable to slap up a simple form and off they go. For me, nothing is that easy. This chapter includes a couple of tips to help spice up your forms and make them a seamless addition to your site. Tutorials included are

- Highlighting Select Boxes
- Fieldset and Legend

Highlighting Select Boxes

Every now and again I run into an effect that I should have known about all the time. It's usually so easy that I'm stunned I think of it. This short tutorial is just such an example.

I was surfing around sites attempting to gather information about a vacation destination when I ran into a site put up by one of the hotels. The site is filled with drop-down boxes. They were just simple drop boxes except the author took the time to add one extra bit of help. He or she highlighted every other choice so that I could easily tell them apart while looking at the numerous choices.

I thought it was a simple, brilliant move. Here's how it was done.

 You can find this tutorial, and all of its examples, online at `http://www.htmlgoodies.com/ tutors/highlightselect.html.`

 You can download just the examples at `http://www.htmlgoodies.com/wpg/.`

Three Examples

Try these on for size! Figure 5.1 shows how the hotel Webmaster simply highlighted every other choice on the site's drop-down menu.

Figure 5.1

Every other level is high-lighted.

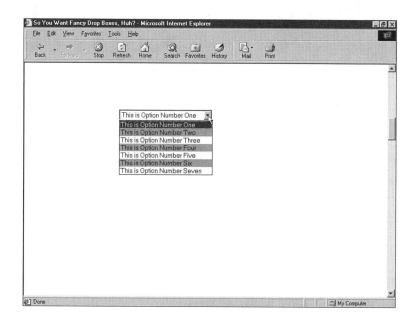

Figure 5.2 shows the same effect, but it uses text color to differentiate instead of selection bars.

Finally here's one I like. Figure 5.3 is a reversal of color. Now the text is white and the background is black.

Okay, so my color choices weren't very good, but I think you can see the good in all this. When you make your color choices, remember that those colors must fit in with your Web site. Don't choose a color simply because it differs from another color so that a line stands out. Always choose your colors with your overall site in mind.

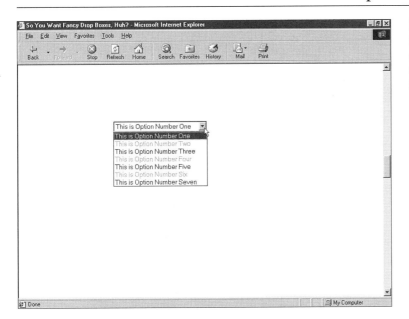

Figure 5.2
Now the text is a different color. It's a little less obvious than the example in Figure 5.1.

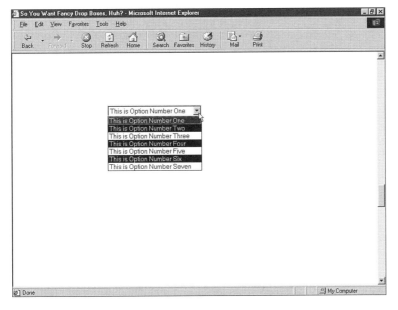

Figure 5.3
Black and white—nice and clean.

As to how much differentiation to put between your lines of code, the rule is, just enough to create the differentiation. Don't go overboard. Just use what you need.

Let's take a look at how it's done. You'll hate that it's so easy.

131

How It's Done

In order to get the effect, you need to understand a little bit about cascading style sheets and classes. The process is this: You set up a class of style sheets, assign a name to it, and then call on that name when you want the effect. Here's all the code from the three preceding boxes plus the Style Sheet block I use to get the effect—I've bolded where I call for the class:

```
<STYLE TYPE="text/css">
.highlight {background:#ff00ff}
.text {color:#ff00ff}
.both {color:white;background:black}
</STYLE>
<FORM>
<SELECT>
<OPTION SELECTED> This is Option Number One
<OPTION CLASS="highlight"> This is Option Number Two
<OPTION> This is Option Number Three
<OPTION CLASS="highlight"> This is Option Number Four
<OPTION> This is Option Number Five
<OPTION CLASS="highlight"> This is Option Number Six
<OPTION> This is Option Number Seven
</SELECT>
</FORM>
<FORM>
<SELECT>
<OPTION SELECTED> This is Option Number One
<OPTION CLASS="text"> This is Option Number Two
<OPTION> This is Option Number Three
<OPTION CLASS="text"> This is Option Number Four
<OPTION> This is Option Number Five
<OPTION CLASS="text"> This is Option Number Six
<OPTION> This is Option Number Seven
</SELECT>
</FORM>
<FORM>
<SELECT>
<OPTION SELECTED> This is Option Number One
<OPTION CLASS="both"> This is Option Number Two
<OPTION> This is Option Number Three
<OPTION CLASS="both"> This is Option Number Four
<OPTION> This is Option Number Five
<OPTION CLASS="both"> This is Option Number Six
<OPTION> This is Option Number Seven
```

```
</SELECT>
</FORM>
```

You create the class in the Style Sheet block with the leading dot. Here's the first one from the preceding:

```
.highlight {background:#ff00ff}
```

This is set to just add a background highlight. Notice that I have the color set to a violet. Now here's how it's called for in the drop box:

```
<OPTION CLASS="highlight"> This is Option Number Two
```

Get it? When you want it, call on it. Take a look at the previous code, and you'll see each of the three classes and how I called for them in the Form code.

It's a great effect with no sweat.

Fieldset and Legend

A lot of commands are proprietary to Internet Explorer. The two I'll discuss here fall under that umbrella. But, unlike many of those proprietary commands, these are basically ignored by Netscape browsers because of placement. They are what I call *ignored* commands. On one browser they do a trick, whereas on the other they do nothing, but also don't hurt anything either. The two commands in this tutorial are both ignored commands.

 You can find this tutorial, and all of its examples, online at `http://www.htmlgoodies.com/ tutors/fieldlegend.html`.

 You can download just the examples at `http://www.htmlgoodies.com/wpg/`.

Figure 5.4 shows an example of what the FIELDSET and LEGEND flags do in a very basic form.

There's not much design to it. It's basic and does the trick. Many people have tried to design their forms by putting them into table cells and putting the cells into an order so that their forms have a nicer look to them. That works fine in Internet Explorer, but certain versions of Netscape don't quite render the table and form correctly because the browser sees tables as individual elements rather than a whole. The use of a table separates the elements. That's not good. Some Netscape browsers tended to mess up the form's output, if not ignore certain sections altogether, because of the table setting.

Figure 5.4
Just a basic form.

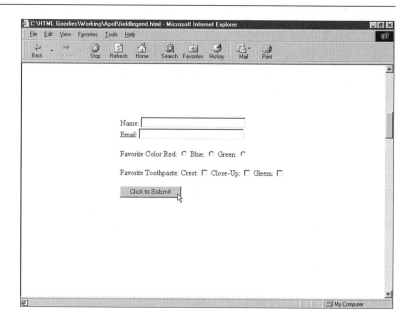

Now, Figure 5.5 displays the same form as previously using the commands we'll hit here.

Figure 5.5
*Wow! My forms have come
alive—in Internet Explorer
at least.*

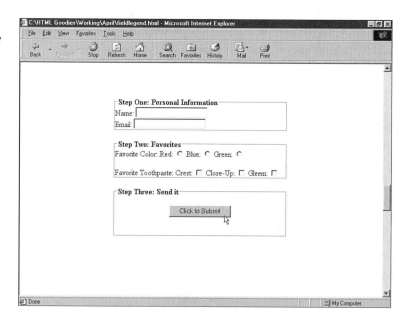

The Flags

Take a good long look at the preceding form. You should be able to get it, and this text, on your screen at the same time. Notice that I grouped elements together by drawing a lined box around them. Remember that you can place as many form elements inside the lined box you want. The elements react to HTML just as they always did: You've just drawn a line around them.

In addition to the line, I've added a title in bold. The title text is placed in the upper left of the lined box by default. I used <B> flags to make the text bold. Now the flags are as follows:

<FIELDSET> drew the lined box. <LEGEND> set the title.

You can pretty much take it from here, but let's take a look at the code that created the first little section surrounding the two text boxes:

```
<FIELDSET>
<LEGEND><b>Step One: Personal Information</b></LEGEND>
Name: <INPUT TYPE="text" SIZE="20">
Email: <INPUT TYPE="text" SIZE="20">
</FIELDSET>
```

<FIELDSET> draws the lined box. <LEGEND> sets the title.

Follow that pattern again and again, grouping form elements as you wish. No sweat!

Use a Table Too

I know this reads like it is in direct contradiction to what I previously wrote about tables and forms, but hear me out. Notice how the FIELDSET table is confined to only 375 pixels wide. It is that way because I surrounded the entire form with a single table cell with the width set to 375. Note that I said a single table cell. That's the key.

It was done purely for aesthetics. If you don't surround the form with a table cell, the lined box runs the length of the browser screen. If there's a way to stop the box from doing that without using a table cell, I couldn't find it. Even examples on the MSIE site showed a table being used to confine the width of the box. My reference book suggests that the attributes ALIGN and WIDTH work with the FIELDSET flag. I tried to get them to work time and time again, but no dice.

Maybe you'll have more luck. Enjoy the commands.

Chapter 6

Helpful Forms

It isn't just important that your forms look good; they also need to provide a service and be helpful for the viewer. This chapter provides the following tips and tricks to enhance your forms to make the user feel better about him or herself:

- Submit When Finished
- Passing Variables with Forms and JavaScript
- Limiting Check Box Choices
- Select Boxes: If This...Then This
- Copy to Clipboard
- Select Box Links Menu
- Hidden Password Protection
- Array Password Protection

Submit When Finished

Okay, form fans, this is one that you've been requesting for a long time now. It's not that I've been ignoring your requests, it's just that...well...okay, I've been ignoring your requests. Sorry! I'm on it now.

Here's the concept: You have a form. You ask your user to fill it in and then submit it. Many of you want the form to submit all by itself when the user presses Enter. I never saw any great benefit to this as part of a guest book form. There are too many items to fill in, and what if the user fills in the last item out of order? Then you'd get a half-finished form submitted. That's not good.

 You can find this tutorial, and all of its examples, online at `http://www.htmlgoodies.com/` `beyond/submitwhendone.html.`

 You can download just the examples at `http://www.htmlgoodies.com/wpg/.`

I'm presenting this tutorial as a single form element submit, like a database search or a simple email or name submit. You can see those all over the place now because everyone wants to put out a newsletter, including me. The single form element is there to capture the user's email to add it to the list of those getting the newsletter.

Figure 6.1 shows an example of what I'm talking about.

Figure 6.1
This is the basic form you'll get. Notice that there is no Submit button.

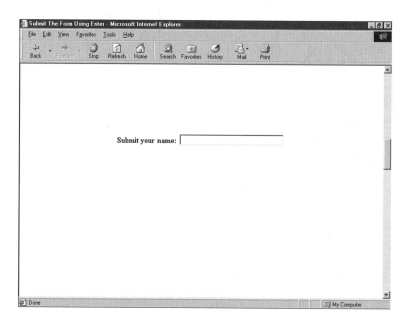

The Code

The code is a short form coupled with an even shorter JavaScript. It looks like this:

```
<SCRIPT LANGUAGE="javascript">
function send()
{document.theform.submit()}
</SCRIPT>
<FORM NAME="theform" METHOD="post"
```

```
ACTION="mailto:jburns@htmlgoodies.com"
➥ENCTYPE="text/plain">
<b>Submit your Name:</b>
<INPUT TYPE="text" name="mardi" size="30"
MAXLENGTH="30" onUnfocus="send()">
</FORM>
```

The Form Code

We'll start with the form code.

The form code is no different than any other form you've created before. The `form` tag offers a NAME, a METHOD, and then the ACTION. I have this one set to work as a simple `mailto:` form, but it can just as easily work by attaching the output to a CGI. Just put the path to the CGI right there after the ACTION, like you normally would. The name of the form is `"theform"`. How's that for originality, huh?

The INPUT TYPE is a text box. Its NAME is `"mardi"`. It's set to a `size` of 30 and a `maxlength` of 30.

The next snippet of text is the clincher. See that `onUnfocus="send()"`? That's what triggers the JavaScript to run and send the form.

The form, of course, wraps up with the required `</FORM>` tag.

The JavaScript Code

Here it is one more time:

```
<SCRIPT LANGUAGE="javascript">
function send()
{document.theform.submit()}
</SCRIPT>
```

The script is super simple. It's a function triggered by the `onUnfocus` Event Handler in the form element. Remember that? The command `onUnfocus` works when focus is taken off an element. You probably could have guessed that. What is the movement that takes focus away from the form element? Why, it's the user pressing Enter. See how it all works?

After focus has been put on and then taken off the text box, the line `document.theform.submit()` fires up. This is the hierarchy line that takes the content of something called "theform" and submits it as if you clicked a submit button.

That's really all there is to it.

You can pretty much plop this on your page anywhere you want it, but I would suggest putting the function up in the head commands if you can.

This is a clever trick, but remember that you might run into trouble if you use it as part of a larger script. Stick with single elements like I showed previously, and you'll do just fine.

Passing Variables with Forms and JavaScript

One of the big questions people have is how they can carry information across pages. User A makes a choice on one page and then goes to another. How can I "remember" what her choice was? Well, the best way is to set a cookie. The cookie is placed right on the user's computer and can be recalled again and again. I have a tutorial on doing just that right here.

The problem is that many people are scared of cookies. They don't like them and feel they're an invasion of their privacy. Okay, that's fine. So now how do I get information across pages? Well, you could do it through one page spawning another, and then another, and then another. That would allow JavaScript variables to be transferred, but that opens a lot of windows.

To attempt to solve this little dilemma, I offer this down-and-dirty JavaScript method.

 You can find this tutorial, and all of its examples, online at `http://www.htmlgoodies.com/ beyond/jspass.html`.

 You can download just the examples at `http://www.htmlgoodies.com/wpg/`.

I'll need two screen captures to show this effect. Figure 6.2 shows the form. Notice that I have put in my first and last name.

Figure 6.3 shows the next page after clicking the button. The values in those two text boxes have been plucked out and used to create the text of the page.

How It Works

Let me start by showing you the code that made the small form in Figure 6.2:

```
<FORM METHOD="LINK" ACTION="jspass2.html">
Type your first name: <INPUT TYPE="text" NAME="FirstName">
Type your last name: <INPUT TYPE="text" NAME="LastName">
<INPUT TYPE="submit" VALUE="Click and See">
</FORM>
```

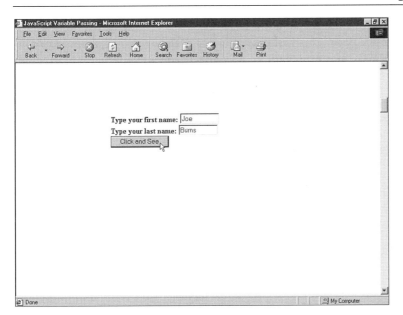

Figure 6.2
Ready to go.

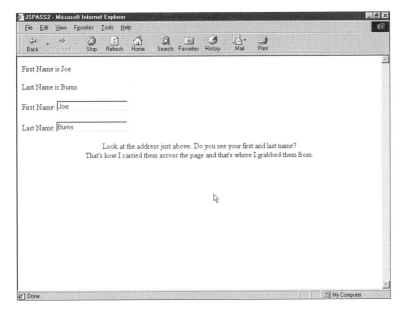

Figure 6.3
Now that's a pretty cool trick. No cookies were used or harmed in the making of this effect.

Look first at the main FORM flag. The METHOD is set to LINK, and the ACTION simply points toward another page. Nowhere does it say to send the user information anywhere. When you set up the form in this manner, the user input is carried along in the URL. This format does not require that the form be given a name. We are not interested in the form as a whole. We want the text from the individual text boxes.

The information is separated from the actual address by a question mark, so it doesn't harm the movement to another page. This little quirk of the browser allows us to go to a totally new page and carry the user's input right along with us in the URL.

Pretty clever, yes? Now all we have to do is find a method of extracting that information from the URL.

Limitations

Now might be a darn good time to discuss limitations to this process.

To begin with, the information is not saved after each surfing like it is with a cookie. In order for this to work, you must ensure that the user moves in a linear fashion. Returning and backing up can harm the information being carried.

Next, the way I have this set up, you can only transfer two variables from page to page. You'll see why in a moment.

Also, the method I have written here isn't very friendly to spaces. If the user puts a space in either of her two text boxes, that space will be replaced by a plus sign. If you're going to accept spaces, you'll either have to live with that or write some extra code to eliminate it.

In addition, this is done with JavaScript, so there are browsers that will not be able to play with it. I have written my code in JavaScript 1.0 so that most browsers can understand what is to happen. I saw a suggestion on doing this by setting the answers to an array. It's clever coding, but it's in JavaScript 1.2, which means bunches of browsers will throw errors. The array method allows for endless variables being passed but limited browsers. Mine allows for the most number of browsers to be able to play with the code but only two variables. You decide.

Get the First Name

Okay, because you've obviously chosen my method (or else you probably wouldn't be reading this far), let's look at the code that grabs the first name. This code will be found on the page that the previous form IS GOING TO

```
<FORM NAME="joe">
<INPUT TYPE="hidden" NAME="burns">
</FORM>
<SCRIPT LANGUAGE="javascript">
var locate = window.location
document.joe.burns.value = locate
var text = document.joe.burns.value
function delineate(str)
{
```

```
theleft = str.indexOf("=") + 1;
theright = str.lastIndexOf("&");
return(str.substring(theleft, theright));
}
document.write("First Name is " +delineate(text));
</SCRIPT>
```

I'm going to tell you up front the hardest part of this process. It kept me at bay for a good hour. I knew that the easiest method for doing this was to use substring JavaScript commands and grab elements from the URL. I also knew that I could grab the URL of a page simply by using the command `window.location`. Here is the URL of the online page using the command: `http://www.htmlgoodies.com/beyond/jspass.html`.

It's no sweat, right? There's the text string. Just grab what you want. The problem is that display is not a text string. It's a property, which means that it cannot be acted on like a text string. Oh, that drove me nuts. After I figured out how to get it from a property to a text string, I was fine. Let's look at that part first.

Okay, JavaScript friends, I know that there are other ways of doing this; this is just how I like to do it. The code starts with this:

```
<FORM NAME="joe">
<INPUT TYPE="hidden" NAME="burns">
</FORM>
```

You might remember that little blip of code for any number of forms you put together. It's basically a text box, but it's hidden. See how the type is `"hidden"`? That's a great little trick to give yourself a place to store a value where no one can see it.

I figured if I take the property of the page's location and put it in a text box, the property then becomes the value of that text box. When you grab the value from a text box, it becomes…you guessed it…a text string. Let's look at the script:

```
var locate = window.location
document.joe.burns.value = locate
var text = document.joe.burns.value
```

That's the beginning blip of code that changes the location into a text string. The property `window.location` is given to a variable named `locate`. Then the value of `locate` is put into the text box represented by `document.joe.burns.value`. See that in the code snippet? The NAME of the form itself is `joe`, and the NAME or the hidden text box is `burns`. By adding `value` to the end of the hierarchy statement, I basically forced a value in to the box.

The next line grabs that value out of the hidden text box and assigns the variable name text to it. The location of the page is now a text string and ready to be broken into parts.

Let's say that it looks like this:

```
http://www.server.com/jspass2.html?FirstName=Super&LastName=Man
```

In order to grab things out of this line of code, we need to look for key elements looking from left to right and later, right to left. In the preceding example, we want the text Super yanked out of this line of letters.

The keys would most likely be the equal sign (=); it's the first one counting from the left. The ending key would be the ampersand (&). Again, it's the first one looking from the left. That bookends the text, so let's set up a JavaScript that knocks everything off including that equals sign and keeps the next letters until an ampersand shows up. It's not too hard:

```
function delineate(str)
{
theleft = str.indexOf("=") + 1;
theright = str.lastIndexOf("&");
return(str.substring(theleft, theright));
}
document.write("First Name is " +delineate(text));
```

First a function, named delineate(), is set up that will look for certain things.

The variable theleft is given the value of the first instance of an equals sign reading from the left. That's what indexOf()does. Notice that we add one because we don't want the equals sign. Adding one skips it. Notice that each line is acting on something called str. At the moment, str has no value. We'll pass it a value in the last line.

Next, the variable theright is given the value of looking for the first instance of & reading from the right. That's what lastIndexOf() does.

So now we have our bookends set. Let's grab the text. The next line returns the substring of what appears between the equals sign (theleft) and the & (theright). See that?

Finally, the value is grabbed using a document.write command. Remember that at this point, nothing has actually been done. The document.write statement actually triggers the function to run. But look! When the function is triggered to run, now it is being passed a new variable, text. That's the text string of the location to be acted on.

The return is the text Super.

Grab the Last Name

Grabbing the last name is a whole lot easier. If you look at the text string again, you'll see that we only need to set one point to look for. Nothing follows the last name, so if we read from the right and basically chop off everything including the second equal sign (from the right, it's the first), we'll be left with the last name. Here's the code that did it:

```
var locate = window.location
document.joe.burns.value = locate
var text = document.joe.burns.value
function delineate2(str)
{
point = str.lastIndexOf("=");
return(str.substring(point+1,str.length));
}
document.write("Last Name is " +delineate2(text));
```

The code is very much the same in that it grabs the `window.location` and turns it into text. Where it differs is that the text string is only searching, from the right, for one item—the second equal sign.

The variable `point` is given the job of representing everything up to the second equal sign (first from the right—note I used `lastIndexOf()`).

The return is that point plus one, again to not include the equal sign, and then the length of the string—that's everything that follows and that's the last name.

A `document.write` statement again triggers the function and passes the variable `text` to it.

Placing the Value

At this point in time, you can place the value anywhere you want by using the `document.write` wherever you want. I have some text thrown in, but that's easily taken out. Remember to remove the plus sign if you take out the text. Getting the name into a text box is actually pretty easy. Here's the code I used on the example page:

```
<FORM NAME="bull">
Last Name: <INPUT TYPE="text" NAME="bear">
</FORM>
<SCRIPT LANGUAGE="javascript">
var zork = delineate2(text)
document.bull.bear.value = zork
</SCRIPT>
```

You might notice a big chunk of it from the other scripts. I created a box first. The box has to be first, or the hierarchy statement won't run, producing an error. The box is visible this time around. The value of the function is assigned to the variable zork, and then zork is put in to the text box. That's pretty straightforward.

Just remember to change out the NAMEs of each element if you put more than one text box on a page. You also have to come up with a different variable name for the second text box. In other words, you can't have two zorks on the same page.

And speaking of two zorks on the same page, remember the limitations of this. You can carry the same info across many pages, but they all must be in order. If you take these variables to yet a third page, all this coding must be redone on the new page. The variable does not carry across pages. The text in the URL carries. After it gets to the new page, it has to be assigned a new variable—each time.

Limiting Check Box Choices

Here's a fantastic effect. As you know, multiple check boxes are often avoided in forms because users have a tendency to simply check all the boxes no matter what. Radio buttons have become the preferred element when a choice must be made. You mostly see check boxes used as single items. I see them mostly at the end of larger forms asking if I want to receive a newsletter or email updates about a product I'm downloading.

But what if you want a user to choose two out of, say, five elements?

 You can find this tutorial, and all of its examples, online at http://www.htmlgoodies.com/tutors/onlytwo.html.

 You can download just the examples at http://www.htmlgoodies.com/wpg/.

Well, here's a script you can attach to your forms that will allow you to limit the number of checks your users can make. You'll fall in love with check boxes all over again. I got the original idea for this script from The Codeman. He has a similar script that only worked in Internet Explorer. I took the concept and rewrote it so that the script would work across browsers.

Here's the effect shown in Figure 6.4. I know that it says to choose only two, but in order to see the effect, I picked a third. I say go ahead! Break the rules! Try to pick three!

You can even make different choices, unclick choices, and change things around. As long as you only have two, you're good to go. Choose three, and you get the alert.

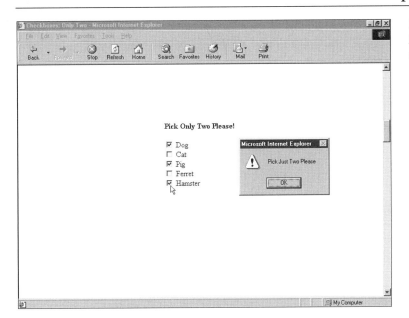

Figure 6.4
But I want three...I'm a rebel!

Did you see it? Not only did you get that nasty alert window, but you also had your third choice unclicked. Take that! Of course you can set the script to allow as many or as few clicks as you'd like, but in order to do that you need to understand how this puppy works. So let's get into it.

The Form Elements

I only have check boxes in the example, but you can surround them with any number of extra form elements. I just singled out the form check boxes for demonstration purposes. The code looks like this:

```
<FORM NAME="joe">
<b>Pick Only Two Please!</b>
<INPUT TYPE="checkbox" NAME="dog"
onClick="return KeepCount()"> Dog
<INPUT TYPE="checkbox" NAME="cat"
onClick="return KeepCount()"> Cat
<INPUT TYPE="checkbox" NAME="pig"
onClick="return KeepCount()"> Pig
<INPUT TYPE="checkbox" NAME="ferret"
onClick="return KeepCount()"> Ferret
<INPUT TYPE="checkbox" NAME="hamster"
onClick="return KeepCount()"> Hamster
</FORM>
```

147

These are basic check boxes. The form is named "joe". Each check box is then given a NAME. The NAME is equal to what the check box represents. That's pretty basic form stuff.

The trick is the onClick() inside each of the check boxes. Notice the onClick() asks for a return from a function named KeepCount(). That return function will allow us to disallow the third box (or whichever you choose) to be checked.

Make a point of following that format or this JavaScript won't give you the desired effect.

Got it? Super! Let's move along...

The Script

It's a fairly simple little script. It looks like this:

```
<SCRIPT LANGUAGE="javascript">
function KeepCount() {
var NewCount = 0
if (document.joe.dog.checked)
{NewCount = NewCount + 1}
if (document.joe.cat.checked)
{NewCount = NewCount + 1}
if (document.joe.pig.checked)
{NewCount = NewCount + 1}
if (document.joe.ferret.checked)
{NewCount = NewCount + 1}
if (document.joe.hamster.checked)
{NewCount = NewCount + 1}
if (NewCount == 3)
{
alert('Pick Just Two Please')
document.joe; return false;
}
}
</SCRIPT>
```

The script works because it's set up to inspect every check box every time. That's how you're able to check, uncheck, and check again as long as only two are checked. The script counts the number of check marks every time you click.

We start with the function. I called it KeepCount() for fairly obvious reasons. You'll remember that this function will trigger every time your user chooses a check box.

We need to give the JavaScript somewhere to keep a count, so I set it up as a variable named NewCount.

Now comes the magic. Notice that the script checks each check box right in a row, every time. Here's just the first blip of code:

```
if (document.joe.dog.checked)
{NewCount = NewCount + 1}
```

If the first check box (dog) is checked, NewCount gets one added to it. If not, we move along to the next check box. Following the script down, if cat is checked, one is added. If not, we go to the next blip.

Each check box is tested in order. The script keeps count again and again each time the user clicks. But what happens if three are checked:

```
if (NewCount == 3)
{
alert('Pick Just Two Please')
document.joe; return false;
}
```

If NewCount is equal (==) to 3, up pops the alert box and then returns to the form; thus the third check box is false. It unclicks.

Cool, huh? The function bracket and the end-script flag round out the script.

The reason that the script is able to count the boxes again and again is way at the top of the function. Note that every time the function triggers, the NewCount value is set back to 0.

You can set this to as many check boxes as you'd like and as many choices from those boxes as you'd like. If you use the effect more than once on a page, please remember that you must change out the NAME of the check boxes, so you must also change out the names in the script.

You'll need a blip of code for every check box you have in order for the check boxes to count each time. Just make sure that your script equals your check boxes both in number and in NAMEs. My suggestion is, if you're going to use this more than one time on the page, paste an entirely new script with a new function name and new count name other than NewCount.

Just make sure to keep the return command in the check boxes themselves. That's what makes the magic in this little script.

Select Boxes: If This...Then This

Okay, so I'm zipping around the Web looking for the answer to a coding question. I didn't find the answer I was looking for there, but I did find a lot of other neat stuff.

You can find this tutorial, and all of its examples, online at *http://www.htmlgoodies. comtutors/ifthis.html.*

 You can download just the examples at *http://www.htmlgoodies.com/wpg/.*

The scripts I found on the sites I viewed were pretty good, so I took a couple of ideas in order to make an easy to incorporate script in to a Web page. Now, in order to see the effect, you have to be running Internet Explorer 5.0 or better or a later version of Netscape. Dig this.

Figure 6.5 shows the form set before anything was done to it. No choices were made yet.

Figure 6.5
Looks like a normal form...

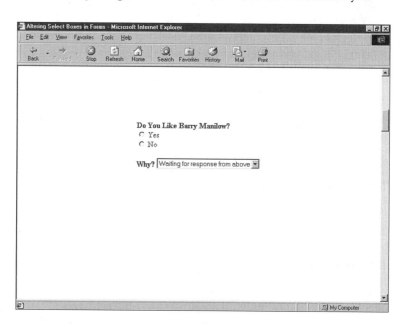

Figure 6.6 shows the same form after the Yes answer was chosen. Note that the choices in the select box have changed.

Figure 6.7 shows how choosing No just pushes the user along. But then, who doesn't like Barry? I do.

Cool, huh? I only have the effect running on one select box at the moment, but I think you can see the advantage of the effect. How many times have you run into a static form that asked questions that didn't apply? Now you can create a form that will react to the user's responses. Depending on what the user enters, you can grab more information or simply tell the user to move on to the next question.

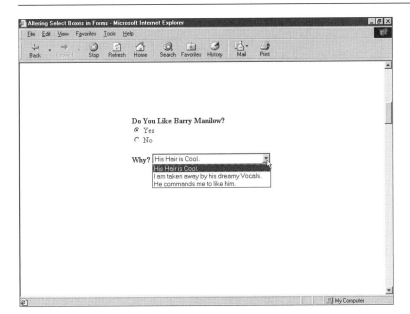

Figure 6.6
It's the hair, isn't it?

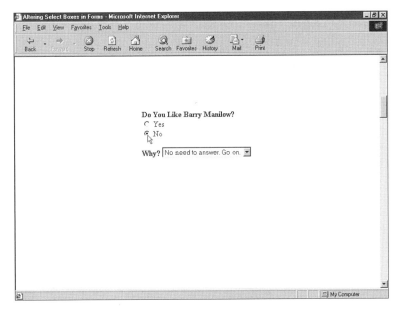

Figure 6.7
*Oh, just go on. You'll learn
to love him!*

The Form Code

Here is the basic code:

```
<FORM NAME="joe">
<b>Do You Like Barry Manilow?</b>
<INPUT TYPE="radio" NAME="zork" VALUE="yes"
➥onClick="YesAnswer()"> Yes
<INPUT TYPE="radio" NAME="zork" VALUE="no"
➥onClick="NoAnswer()"> No
<b>Why? </b> <SELECT NAME="burns">
<OPTION SELECTED> Waiting for response from above
</SELECT>
</FORM>
```

The form is named "joe". The radio buttons are both named "zork" so that no matter which is chosen, the effect will trigger. The select box is named "burns". I often name form elements with my own name. It just helps me remember the element names without having to go back and look again and again. (That doesn't explain the "zork" though, does it?)

The form is very basic except that the select box only has one element. The reason is that more would be silly. I'm going to change the content no matter which button the user chooses, so why go on and add multiple responses?

Notice that if the Yes radio button is clicked, YesAnswer() is triggered. If the No button is clicked, NoAnswer() is triggered. OK! We're done here. We're moving along...

The Script Code

The script code is a little lengthy, but stay with me here. You'll note that it's just the same thing again and again. Most scripts are like that.

```
<'SCRIPT LANGUAGE="JavaScript">

function YesAnswer()
{
var IntPath = document.joe.burns;
var TheOptions = IntPath.options.length;

document.joe.burns.options.length = 0;

IntPath.options[IntPath.options.length] =
new Option('His Hair is Cool','0');
IntPath.options[IntPath.options.length] =
new Option('I am taken away by his dreamy Vocals','1');
```

```
IntPath.options[IntPath.options.length] =
new Option('He commands me to like him','2');
}

function NoAnswer()
{
var IntPath = document.joe.burns;
var TheOptions = IntPath.options.length;

document.joe.burns.options.length = 0;

IntPath.options[IntPath.options.length] = new Option
➧('No Need to Answer. Go On. ','0');
}

</SCRIPT>
```

Place the script from the new window into your HTML document. In between the HEAD flags is best, but it'll basically run from anywhere as long as it sits above the form in the document. That's a Netscape thing.

Notice that the script is in two sections. The first is a function for YesAnswer(), and the second is a function for NoAnswer(). Can you see it all coming together now?

I've set two variables:

```
var IntPath = document.joe.burns;
var TheOptions = IntPath.options.length;
```

The first, IntPath represents the initial path to the select box. It follows the path document, and then the form name, and then the form element name.

The second variable, TheOptions uses the IntPath but also adds the additional directions options (the elements in the select box) and length (the number of options in the select box).

The next line reads

```
document.joe.burns.options.length = 0;
```

This line's only purpose is to clear what is currently written in the select box so that new text can be written. If we didn't have this, the new text would simply be written under the existing text. That would be rather confusing, don't you think? Well, now that we've blanked the select box, we might as well write something in there:

153

```
IntPath.options[IntPath.options.length] =
➥new Option('His Hair is Cool','0');
IntPath.options[IntPath.options.length] =
➥new Option('I am taken away by his dreamy Vocals','1');
IntPath.options[IntPath.options.length] =
➥new Option('He commands me to like him','2');
```

If you simply keep in mind what IntPath represents (document.joe.burns), this reads pretty easily. In the select box's options, write this new option. Then you receive the text for the new option and the option's array number. Remember that JavaScript starts counting at zero, not one. That's why the first new option's number is 0. Numbers 1 and 2 follow right along.

If you click on the Yes radio button, the function YesAnswer() runs and the preceding script is enacted. If you click the No button, the NoAnswer()function triggers and the same process runs, yet only one option is entered in the box. That option's sole purpose is to tell the user to go on to the next question, so only one option is needed.

Multiple Form Elements

Because most forms do not have a single drop-down box like this one, you'll need to know how to alter this script if you have multiple form elements. My suggestion is to not get overly fancy with the coding. Create a new set of functions for each form/select box grouping you create.

That means a simple copy and paste, but be careful, you'll need to change a few things. For one, the form elements will have new names, so you'll have to change not only the name of the function, but also the name of the select box in the script.

So...

Change the name of the function in the form element itself so that each radio button grouping triggers a function built specifically for its purpose. That means you'll have to change the name both in the script (when you paste in a new function) and in the form itself.

In the script, you'll need to change the name of the select box element. That means everywhere you see burns (the name of the current select box), you'll need to change the name to the new select box.

It'll create a lot of text, that's for sure, but you'll be able to keep it all straight if you follow this format.

Using this script format can make a great form that will actually interact with the user rather than bothering the user by asking questions that shouldn't be answered. I'm not a fan of surveys that read, "If yes, go here—If no, go here." Using this script, you can alter the questions and answers as the user makes her choices.

Copy to Clipboard

I've seen this effect used in a couple of places. It's a really neat look, so I thought a tutorial would be in order. I grabbed some blips of code and played with it to set it up so that it's an easy grab from a tutorial. You can alter this and pretty it up to your heart's content. All I'm passing along here is the basic code and how it all works. Figure 6.8 shows the foundation for this tutorial.

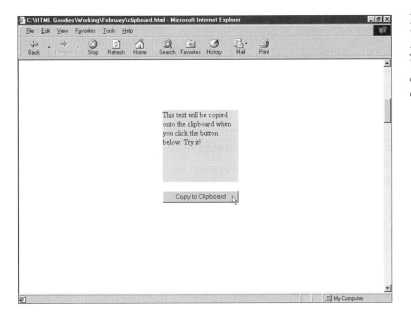

Figure 6.8
This is the basic format you'll get with this tutorial. The text in the box will be copied when the button is clicked.

 You can find this tutorial, and all of its examples, online at `http://www.htmlgoodies.com/beyond/clipboard.html`.

 You can download just the examples at `http://www.htmlgoodies.com/wpg/`.

The Effect

Click the button below the shaded area and then paste it to a text editor. Ta da! That's a cool effect. If I had been able to do this from the beginning, I could have set up every tutorial like this. Well, maybe I wouldn't have. This effect requires the use of a command available only in IE 4.0 or better, `execCommand()`.

It's an Internet Explorer–only statement that allows the browser to execute a command, thus the name. In this case, we're executing a copy. But you'll see the code for that later. Let's talk about what's happening with the visible items first.

I've got a shaded block with text sitting inside. The shading is only there for presentation purposes. It's to show that what is inside of the colored area is what will be copied to the clipboard.

You can't see it yet, but there is also a Textarea box that's hidden. When you click on the button, the program copies the text to the Textarea box and also to the clipboard. Let's take a look at the code that puts these elements to the page.

The Text to Be Copied

Let's start with the code that introduces what is to be copied. Follow this from the top. I have a SPAN surrounding text. That SPAN is given the ID "copytext". Whatever is within the SPAN commands is what will be copied. You'll also note that I popped in an inline STYLE attribute in order to set the SPAN to a specific height, width, and background color. That's not required. I just did it for looks:

```
<SPAN ID="copytext" STYLE="height:150;width:162;background-color:pink">
This text will be copied onto the clipboard
when you click the button below. Try it!
</SPAN>
<TEXTAREA ID="holdtext" STYLE="display:none;">
</TEXTAREA>
<BUTTON onClick="ClipBoard();">Copy to Clipboard</BUTTON>
```

Next is a Textarea box that's been made invisible through an inline STYLE attribute. It has been given the ID "holdtext" because it is there simply to hold the text while copying.

In case you're wondering, I tried the script by changing out NAME for ID, and the JavaScript wouldn't recognize it. I also tried numerous other hidden elements including the traditional INPUT TYPE="hidden", but no dice. It really doesn't matter though because this works well.

Finally, a basic button is in place simply to trigger the JavaScript that performs the copy. Yes, you can go with the traditional FORM button. That doesn't matter. The button only triggers the function, ClipBoard().

The JavaScript

The script uses a lot of commands proprietary to Internet Explorer 4.0 and above. You'll want to be careful about changing any text you think might be a simple variable name.

Except for the two names we assigned, `holdtext` and `copytext`, as well as `Copied` within the script itself, everything else carries with it actions past just a name. That's why the script is so functional yet is so small. Let's take it from the top...

```
<SCRIPT LANGUAGE="JavaScript">
function ClipBoard()
{
holdtext.innerText = copytext.innerText;
Copied = holdtext.createTextRange();
Copied.execCommand("Copy");
}
</SCRIPT>
```

The function is named `ClipBoard()`. It is triggered when the button is clicked. The text that appears within (`innerText`) the `Textarea` box (`holdtext`) is created by taking the text from within (`innerText`) the `SPAN` (`copytext`).

Parameters are set around that text (`holdtext.createTextRange()`), and the text is given a name (`Copied`).

Next, the text (`Copied`) is copied to the clipboard using the IE `execCommand` to copy.

That's about it in a nutshell.

What If There Is Code?

The script, as it is currently written, copies whatever text is within the `SPAN` flags. If there is code, like a `<BR>` command created to display using & commands, those will copy right along. If you have formatting in the text and you only want the user to copy the text, you need to add a command that will remove that formatting. Luckily, there's an `execCommand` that will do that for you. It's important that you place it in the script before the copy process.

The script will look like this:

```
<SCRIPT LANGUAGE="JavaScript">
function ClipBoard()
{
holdtext.innerText = copytext.innerText;
Copied = holdtext.createTextRange();
Copied.execCommand("RemoveFormat");
Copied.execCommand("Copy");
}
</SCRIPT>
```

157

I made the new line bold so it would stick out a little more. That line will remove any formatting associated with the copied code, so just the text will copy.

Multiple Copies on One Page

As with any time a JavaScript sits on a page, if you post multiples of that JavaScript, you need to make a point of changing the variables that attach the visible elements with the JavaScript. In this case, that includes the name of the function, the ID of the SPAN, the ID of the hidden Textarea box, and the variable name you give in the script itself to represent the text. I used "Copied".

This is a great effect, and it will work with voluminous amounts of text or just a few words. This script goes to the concept of interacting with the user. Instead of asking the user to copy and paste, now you can help her along in the process by doing at least the copy for her.

Select Box Links Menu

This tutorial is a series of basic drop-down link menus. I remember very well when this form of creating links came out. Everyone wanted to know how to do it. Because of that, everyone tried at once, and many different methods of getting a FORM-based drop-down menu to act as links started floating around the Web. This is a very basic format. I think it's a good one, but just keep in mind that this certainly isn't the only way of getting the job done.

 You can find this tutorial, and all of its examples, online at *http://www.htmlgoodies.com/ stips/scripttip38.html.*

 You can download just the examples at *http://www.htmlgoodies.com/wpg/.*

As you'll see, this link menu uses a button to trigger its effect. That can be eliminated, and after we understand how this format works, we'll alter the script a bit so that the button isn't required. It'll just make the link when the user chooses from the menu.

This format works outside of frames. After the no-button version, we'll alter it again so that it works within a frames format by loading its URLs into a separate frames window. Basically, we're going to beat this drop-down menu to death.

Figure 6.9 is a look at the first version of this navigation system.

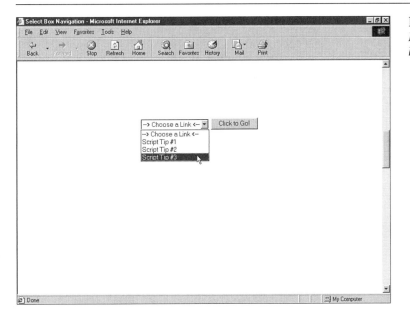

Figure 6.9
*Pull the menu, click the
button, and wheeeeeee!*

The Script

Here's the entire script:

```
<SCRIPT LANGUAGE="javascript">
function LinkUp()
{
var number = document.DropDown.DDlinks.selectedIndex;
location.href = document.DropDown.DDlinks.options
➥ [number].value;
}
</SCRIPT>
<FORM NAME="DropDown">
<SELECT NAME="DDlinks">
<OPTION SELECTED>--> Choose a Link <--
<OPTION VALUE="scripttip1.html"> Page One
<OPTION VALUE="scripttip2.html"> Page Two
<OPTION VALUE="scripttip3.html"> Page Three
</SELECT>
<INPUT TYPE="BUTTON" VALUE="Click to Go!"
➥onClick="LinkUp()">
</FORM>
```

We'll get underway by once again starting from the bottom up. Here's the HTML that creates the drop-down box and the button:

```
<FORM NAME="DropDown">
<SELECT NAME="DDlinks">
<OPTION SELECTED>--> Choose a Link <--
<OPTION VALUE="scripttip1.html"> Page One
<OPTION VALUE="scripttip2.html"> Page Two
<OPTION VALUE="scripttip3.html"> Page Three
</SELECT>
<INPUT TYPE="BUTTON" VALUE="Click to Go!"
➥onClick="LinkUp()">
</FORM>
```

You should be quite familiar with the drop-down link format by now. We start by setting a FORM and giving it a name. This form will be named DropDown. See that in the code?

Next, we'll set up the select box and give it a name. We'll call this one DDlinks. Are you still with me?

The first "option" is the one that will display, so we will not give that a VALUE. It will display the following text:

```
"--> Choose a link <--".
```

Next, we start listing the options that will be used to create links. Each is given a VALUE that represents the link it will point toward. Now, I only have that page name because the files I'm linking to are in the same directory. If you want to set this to links outside of your site, just put the entire URL in for the VALUE. For instance:

```
<OPTION VALUE="http://www.htmlgoodies.com/new.html">
```

I have three items to choose from. You can have 50 or more, if you want. I'm just keeping it small for the example.

The </SELECT> ends the drop-down box.

The button comes next:

```
<INPUT TYPE="BUTTON" VALUE="Click to Go!"
➥onClick="LinkUp()">
```

Its job is to trigger the function that will grab the VALUE and turn it into a link. See the onClick="LinkUp()"? That's what will do it.

Finally, </FORM> wraps up the FORM elements of this script's HTML side. Now that we know the players, we can go after the function.

The Function

This is what we're interested in:

```
function LinkUp()
{
var number = document.DropDown.DDlinks.selectedIndex;
location.href = document.DropDown.DDlinks.options
➡ [number].value;
}
```

See how the long lines of code should stay on one written line?

That's the format. If you change it from that, you'll get errors. The entire script, a little higher up on the page, truncates the second line. That's bad. Keep it all on one line.

The function is named `LinkUp()` for no other reason than that's what I've chosen. It's a name I completely made up. Then comes the curly bracket that will surround the function commands. Then comes the first line of the function itself:

```
var number = document.DropDown.DDlinks.selectedIndex;
```

This first line assigns a variable name, `number`, to the value returned from the drop-down menu. Remember, the name of the form is `DropDown`, the name of the select box itself is `DDlinks`, and the value chosen by the user is represented in JavaScript by `selectedIndex`.

Now you have the number chosen by the user returned and assigned to the variable number. Just keep in mind that JavaScript counts everything, and it starts counting at zero. So the first choice, the zero choice, is no good. That's the one that reads "Choose a Link."

Now here's the second line of the function:

```
location.href = document.DropDown.DDlinks.options
➡ [number].value;
```

You might remember "`location.href`" as the JavaScript that creates a hypertext link. If not, that's what it does. The link then is created by gathering the VALUE from the choice the user has made.

Once again, a hierarchy statement is created using the name of the form, the name of the select box, and then `option[number]`.

That `[number]` is the variable name we just created. It represents the hierarchy statement that will grab the number of the drop-down box the user chose. Thus when this script runs, the text "number" will actually be replaced with the number the user chose. Because this drop-down box only offers three choices (past the zero choice "Choose a Link"), that number will be 1, 2, or 3.

161

After the script replaces number with an actual number, it then asks for the VALUE. And what is the value for each OPTION? It's a hypertext link!

The script grabs that hypertext link VALUE and the location.href creates the link. Ta da! That's pretty clever. However, the link does not actually happen until the function is triggered to work. That happens through the button's onClick="LinkUp()" Event Handler statement. See that in the preceding code?

But what if we could set it up so that the button wasn't needed? The user simply made her choice, and the link went off immediately. Wouldn't that be cool?

No Button

Figure 6.10 shows the effect we're going for next. It's the same navigation format, but this time around it just happens. No buttons are required.

Figure 6.10
Pull the menu, let go, and wheeeeeee!

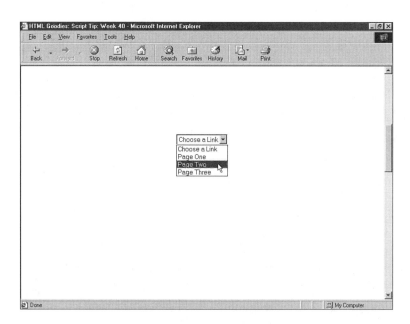

This is a rather easy effect to generate. Notice that the button code has been taken out. The function remains the same, as does the code for the drop-down box itself. Here's the new code that does the trick:

```
<SELECT NAME="DDlinks" onChange="LinkUp(this.form)">
```

An Event Handler, onChange, is used to fire the function, LinkUp(). onChange works just as you think it does. As soon as something changes, it's triggered. When the page loads, the

OPTION SELECTED is the item displayed. When someone changes that, the function is triggered.

This hasn't come up a lot in the Script Tips, but do you see the text within the instance (the parentheses)? That text is known as a "parameter." In this case, it is information that is going to be passed to the function.

The information passed to the function couldn't be more clear, this.form. The output of the form, the index number of the user's choice, is sent up to the function and used, along with the VALUE, to create the hypertext link just as it was when we had the button.

Here's one more thing. Notice where I placed the onChange Event Handler? It is in the SELECT flag, not the first OPTION flag. That's because the SELECT will change. The first OPTION will always stay the same and never trigger the function.

It sounds easy enough, but will it work across frames? Sure, it will!

Across Frames

Ever since I announced we would be playing around with this drop-down menu, the mail has been coming in saying, "When are you going to get to the configuration that allows me to use this across frames?" Wait no longer. We're there. Figures 6.11 and 6.12 show this script's latest configuration.

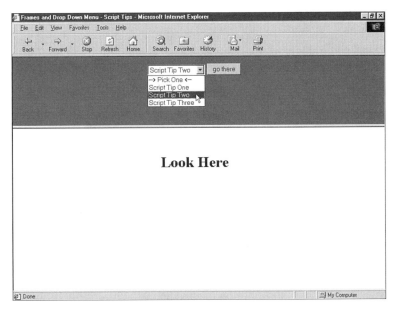

Figure 6.11
Pull the menu, click the button, cross the frame, and...

Figure 6.12
Wheeeeeee!

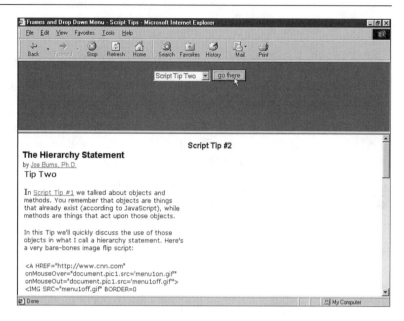

The Code

You sharp-eyed readers will notice that I brought the button back. If you want to be rid of it, reread the last tutorial and follow the same format. For this across-frames format, I want the button. Here we go:

```
<SCRIPT LANGUAGE="JavaScript">
function acrossFrames()
{
if (document.FrameForm.DDFrameForm.options[0].selected)
parent.frames[0].location='menuframes.html'
if (document.FrameForm.DDFrameForm.options[1].selected)
parent.frames[1].location='scripttip1.html'
if (document.FrameForm.DDFrameForm.options[2].selected)
parent.frames[1].location='scripttip2.html'
if (document.FrameForm.DDFrameForm.options[3].selected)
parent.frames[1].location='scripttip3.html'
}
</SCRIPT>
<FORM NAME="FrameForm">
<SELECT NAME="DDFrameForm">
<OPTION SELECTED> --> Pick One <--
<OPTION>Script Tip One
<OPTION>Script Tip Two
```

```
<OPTION>Script Tip Three
</SELECT>
<INPUT TYPE="button" VALUE="go there" onClick="acrossFrames()">
</FORM>
```

Let's start at the bottom. It should look very familiar. The only reason I am showing it to you is that I have changed the name of the form and the drop-down box. It looks like this:

```
<FORM NAME="FrameForm">
<SELECT NAME="DDFrameForm">
<OPTION SELECTED> --> Pick One <--
<OPTION>Script Tip One
<OPTION>Script Tip Two
<OPTION>Script Tip Three
</SELECT>
<INPUT TYPE="button" VALUE="go there" onClick="acrossFrames()">
</FORM>
```

The FORM itself is called "FrameForm" and the SELECT box is named "DDFrameForm". The button is back and is set to trigger a function called acrossFrames(). Let's see the function that passes info from frame window to frame window.

The Function

It looks like this:

```
function acrossFrames()
{
if (document.FrameForm.DDFrameForm.options[0].selected)
parent.frames[0].location='menuframes.html'
if (document.FrameForm.DDFrameForm.options[1].selected)
parent.frames[1].location='scripttip1.html'
if (document.FrameForm.DDFrameForm.options[2].selected)
parent.frames[1].location='scripttip2.html'
if (document.FrameForm.DDFrameForm.options[3].selected)
parent.frames[1].location='scripttip3.html'
}
```

Let me first point out a basic tenant of JavaScript. JavaScript counts everything, and it starts counting at 0. This means that the items in the SELECT box have already been assigned numbers. The first choice is 0, the next choice is 1, and then the choice is 2, and then the choice is 3.

165

In addition to that, the frames have also been given numbers starting at 0. The first frame listed in a page's FRAMESET is frame window 0. The second is frame window 1. The third one listed would be frame window 2, and so on.

The frameset format for the example is a simple two-frame window, in rows, set to 30% and 70%:

```
<FRAMESET ROWS="30%,*">
<FRAME SRC="menuframes.html">
<FRAME SRC="lookhere.html">
</FRAMESET>
```

The first FRAME SRC listed will be known as frames[0]. The second one listed will be known as frames[1]. That's the format of denoting a specific frame in JavaScript hierarchy statements.

Let's look at the first two small blocks of code in the function:

```
if (document.FrameForm.DDFrameForm.options[0].selected)
parent.frames[0].location='menuframes.html'
if (document.FrameForm.DDFrameForm.options[1].selected)
parent.frames[1].location='scripttip1.html'
```

The first choice is the text "Pick One." We do not want that to produce any linking, so I have set that link to reload the same page into the same frame window.

See that? If the item chosen by the user is option[0], the first choice, load menuframes.html in to frames[0], which is the one it is already in. Follow that? It just reloads the same page in the same frame window.

The next block of code is for the second choice. That is choice number 1 because JavaScript starts counting at 0. It reads that if someone chooses options[1], that page is to be loaded into frames[1], the lower frame window. Get it?

Follow along with the next two blocks of code. Each one says that if a specific option is chosen, load it in to frames[1], the lower frame.

Other Frames

But what if you have multiple frames? It's no sweat. Just remember to count your frame windows from 0, top to bottom. If you have five frame windows, they would be numbered 0 through 4. You could set each choice in the drop-down menu to load into a different window simply by putting in the appropriate frame window number.

Each of the function blocks of code is an `If` statement. Usually, an `If` statement ends with an `Else`. This does not because I am sure one of the `If` statements will be true every time someone chooses one of the `SELECT` box items. The `Else` statement is not needed.

You now know more ways to play with a drop-down menu than you will probably ever need to know. So enjoy it. It's a great script that can look very professional on your pages.

Hidden Password Protection

This is the first in a series of two scripts meant to discuss and describe the concept of creating password protection through JavaScript. Each uses a different method of password protection. You choose which one you think is best.

The two are

- Password in script —hidden script
- Password encrypted through arrays

Both are effective to a point. As with most password protection, the protection is only as good as the user's ability to not blab the password. JavaScript has taken a bad rap in all this because many people say that the password is in the script and that it's easy to look at the code, grab the password, and get in.

The second script simply does not include the password, so that's out. The first does, but I'll show you how to make it darn hard to grab it from the code—if you can get to the code at all.

Let's get started with the first one.

Here's the Script

In all honesty, it would do you good to go online and see this pup in action. It's really clever the way the script hides its code.

I have a working copy linked directly to `http://www.htmlgoodies.com/stips/scripttip73effect.html`. Try to break in.

Here's what you're looking for. Figure 6.13 displays the prompt box that's waiting for your password.

The password is "peppermint"—without the quotes. Before you do it correctly, put in incorrect passwords, leave spaces blank, press Cancel, and try to look at the pages code. You'll see how I hid it.

Figure 6.13
What's da' passwoid, bub?

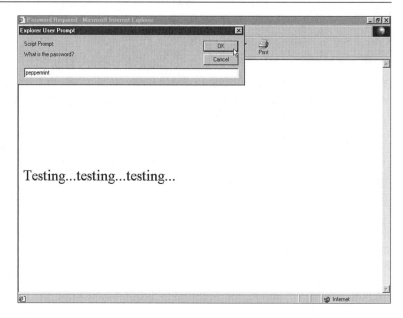

Here's code after you get back:

```
<SCRIPT LANGUAGE="javascript">
var getin = prompt("What is the password?","")
if (getin=="peppermint")
{
alert('You got it! In you go...')
location.href='scripttip73correct.html'
}
else
{
if (getin=="null")
{location.href='nope2.,html'}
else
if (getin!="peppermint")
{location.href='nope.html'}
}
</SCRIPT>
```

How do you like that? I wrote that code for a fellow professor who wanted a basic password system. The system works pretty well, but it is still crack-able if you know how. Did you try to get the password? Hard, wasn't it?

It was difficult because of the way the script was put together. None of the password elements ran before prompt or alert elements. That way, it was impossible to get the page by itself without some type of JavaScript element taking the focus of the browser. The moment you'd click to lose one item, another would pop up.

Let's look at the code:

```
var getin = prompt("What is the password?","")
```

We begin with a prompt that runs first in the script. Every time this page loads, this prompt pops up first. You simply haven't time to get to the view source menu item.

The variable getin is given the value of the text the user puts in to the prompt box.

There's one more thing—notice that there's no text set to go in to the text box part of the prompt. That way, I can set up an event to occur if the user simply clicks Cancel without putting in any text.

```
if (getin=="peppermint")
{
alert('You got it! In you go...')
location.href='scripttip73correct.html'
}
```

The first IF statement is set up to work if the password is correct. If getin is equal (==) to "peppermint" (the password), an alert box pops up. The box is again to keep focus away from the page itself. After you click to close the alert box, the location.href hierarchy statement is enacted and the browser changes the page.

But what if the user puts in the wrong password:

```
else
{
if (getin=="null")
{location.href='nope2.,html'}
else
if (getin!="peppermint")
{location.href='nope.html'}
}
```

The wrong password brings on the wrath of the Else statement. I have the Else statement set to itself to be another If statement. Basically if the user response does not match the original If statement, the user's answer is checked again by a second If statement. The Else moves the user response from one to the other.

If the user just clicks Cancel, the variable `getin` will be null. This response is set to go to a page called `nope2.html` that tells the user to stop clicking Cancel. (NOTE: This doesn't work on all browser versions—but all versions will get the next blip of code.)

If `getin` is not null, a value must be put in by the user. If it is anything but `"peppermint"` (`!=`), the page `nope.html` pops up instructing the user to try again.

That's basically it. It's not a hard script, and the password appears in the code, but it's darn hard to get to. The script creates a vicious circle that can only be broken by putting in the correct password or closing the browser window.

Have you figured out how to get to the code yet? The easiest method is to close the browser and re-open it on the page that would send you to the password page. Then put your pointer on the link, right-click, and download the target page. Then you would have the code and the password.

Had you thought of that? If not, your user might very well not have either. Maybe this password script is the one for you. If what you have to protect isn't of high-end importance, this could be the one.

Array Password Protection

This is the second in a string of JavaScript password scripts. In this script, we again use a format in which the password is the name of the page to be linked to—except in this one, the concept is further hidden because the user will not put in the name of the page. The user will put in a numeric password, which will be turned in to the name of the page by the script.

It's done through an array. It's, again, best if you see this one in action. I have a working version online at `http://www.htmlgoodies.com/stips/scripttip75effect.html`.

Use the password `145`.

The password page looks like Figure 6.14.

Here's the Code

This script creates a very difficult-to-crack password system:

```
<SCRIPT LANGUAGE="javascript">
function GoIn()
{
var Password = new Array("p","j","l","z","o","e","m","b","x","z")
function getNumbers()
{
return document.userInput.u1.value
```

```
return document.userInput.u2.value
return document.userInput.u3.value
}
var input1 = document.userInput.u1.value
var input2 = document.userInput.u2.value
var input3 = document.userInput.u3.value
var pw1 = Password[input1]
var pw2 = Password[input2]
var pw3 = Password[input3]
var pw = pw1 + pw2 + pw3
if (pw == pw1+pw2+pw3)
{location.href = pw+ ".html"}
}
</SCRIPT>
Put in Your Three-Number Password to Enter: <center>
<FORM NAME="userInput">
<INPUT TYPE="text" Name ="u1" SIZE="2">
<INPUT TYPE="text" Name ="u2" SIZE="2">
<INPUT TYPE="text" Name ="u3" SIZE="2">
<INPUT TYPE="button" VALUE="Enter" onClick="GoIn()">
</FORM>
</CENTER>
```

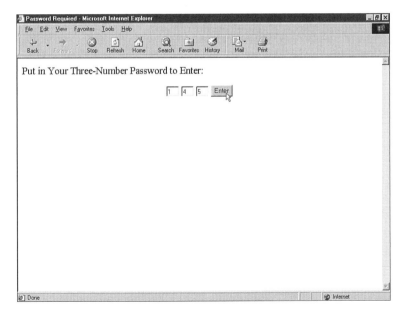

Figure 6.14

Passwords and numbers, and numbers to text.

Of course, when we have form elements in a script, we start with them so that we can understand the hierarchy statements in the functions:

```
<FORM NAME="userInput">
<INPUT TYPE="text" Name ="u1" SIZE="2">
<INPUT TYPE="text" Name ="u2" SIZE="2">
<INPUT TYPE="text" Name ="u3" SIZE="2">
<INPUT TYPE="button" VALUE="Enter" onClick="GoIn()">
</FORM>
```

The form itself is given the name "userInput". Following the form flag are three input text boxes: Each set to accept only two characters.

The text boxes are named "u1", "u2", and "u3" down the line.

A final button triggers a function called GoIn(). Now we can put together hierarchy statement to grab whatever the user puts into the boxes. Now here's the GoIn() function:

```
function GoIn()
{
var Password = new Array("p","j","l","z","o","e","m","b","x","z")
```

The function starts with an array. We've used the format before. The array is named "Password". Each element in the array is a text string because it is contained within double quotes. A comma separates each item, with no spaces.

What isn't shown here is what helps us to use the script as a password function. Any time you set up an array in JavaScript, the array list members are given numbers starting at zero and counting up until JavaScript runs out of things to count.

In this case, "p" is zero, "j" is one, "l" is two, and so forth. That will become important in a moment.

```
function getNumbers() {
return document.userInput.u1.value
return document.userInput.u2.value
return document.userInput.u3.value
}
```

Next, a second function, getNumbers(), is employed to simply return, to the script, the numbers the user put in to the text boxes. Note that the three hierarchy statements are each attached to one of the three text boxes:

```
var input1 = document.userInput.u1.value
var input2 = document.userInput.u2.value
var input3 = document.userInput.u3.value
```

Next, the three input items that are returned from the three text boxes are given the variable names input1, input2, and input3. Please remember that when grabbing values from form elements, the use of the command value is very important at the end of the hierarchy statement.

Here the array is called on three times. (Password is the name assigned to the array, remember?) The array items pulled out will be equal to the three numbers entered by the user. Notice that each time, the variable names assigned to the user's choices are used within square brackets:

```
var pw1 = Password[input1]
var pw2 = Password[input2]
var pw3 = Password[input3]
```

This format works basically like a replacement. Whatever number the user put in will replace the variable name. So if the user put zero in the first box, input1 will be replaced by zero and the first letter of the array, p, will be returned. That happens three times, assigning the variables pw1, pw2, and pw3, for each of the text boxes:

```
var pw = pw1 + pw2 + pw3
if (pw == pw1+pw2+pw3)
{location.href = pw+ ".html"}
}
```

Last but not least, the variable pw is created and given the value of the three variables put together.

An If statement asks if pw is equal to pw1+pw2+pw3. Of course it is. We just set it to that. Because it is, the commands location.href trigger, taking the user to the page name created by the user's three numbers plus .html.

Do that again...

The password for this script is 145. If you count in to the array to 1, you get j. Remember that the p is zero. Count to 4 and you get o. Count one more and you get e.

Put them all together, add .html, and you get the page name "joe.html". If you retry the password, you note that joe.html is the page you were sent to.

Pick the one you like. Each has its own merits, and each can be defeated. I actually like the first one I showed. It's simple, and it works.

Part III

Behind the Scenes

Chapter 7

Your Users Might See These

There are many site options that happen that your users might see and be affected by. This chapter covers the following tips and tricks:

- Placing a Cookie
- Cookie Counter
- Disabling Mouse Clicks
- Minimize and Maximize Buttons
- Refresh the Page
- HTA Files
- Keystroke Captures

Placing a Cookie

This tutorial was really a long time coming. People have wanted it for a while, but I've been somewhat reluctant to write it for a couple of reasons.

First, I knew that as soon as I posted something like this, I would see people setting cookies all over the place. Cookies are very bad in some people's eyes. You can read more about that in my original cookie reference piece. But furthermore, these things are hard!

Setting a cookie using JavaScript, which this tutorial does, can be a real pain in the neck. But now my neck feels fine, and I've written basic cookie-place and cookie-retrieve scripts, so we can move forward.

 You can find this tutorial, and all of its examples, online at `http://www.htmlgoodies.com/beyond/cookie.html`.

 You can download just the examples at `http://www.htmlgoodies.com/wpg/`.

Why Set Cookies?

There are two main reasons that I can think of to set cookies. The first is to "remember" information. Someone comes to your page and offers you his name. Next time, you greet him by that name. This is clever, and it's a nice touch. But then again, many people are wary of cookies and won't feel comfortable accepting a cookie just so you can say "hi" at some later date.

The second reason, and the one I feel is most important, is moving information across pages. Someone chooses something on one page, and when he clicks to go to the next page, what he chose before is now posted there for him. It's the whole basis for a shopping cart program.

My Cookie Script in Action

Any time you set a cookie, you need to gather some information. Usually it's done in the format I'm showing here. Someone enters something into a text box, a button is clicked, and the cookie is written that contains the information provided by the reader.

Once the cookie is written, you can call on it again and again. Figure 7.1 shows the basic format in this tutorial.

Figure 7.2 illustrates what will be shown when you click to go to the next page.

I should tell you up front that, at the moment, the script will not post multiple words in the text box. It's easily fixed, but I'm trying to keep things pretty simple here, so just enter one word.

Setting the Cookie

Yes, it's not that stunning as is, but it gets the point across. If I had you enter your first name, I could have welcomed you again and again each time you arrived. If this were an order form, the next page would have the number you ordered already posted to the page. Get the picture?

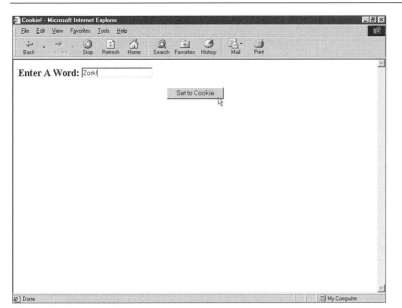

Figure 7.1
I am entering the word "Zork" for no other good reason than I can! So there.

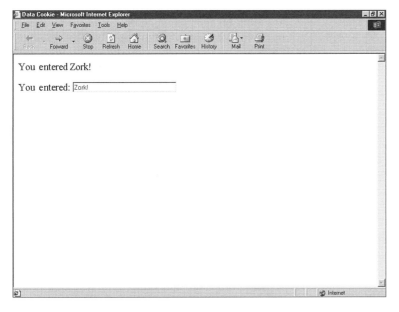

Figure 7.2
Zork appears in two places after reading it from the cookie.

Let's start with the setting of the cookie. It's actually a little easier than the retrieval:

```
<SCRIPT LANGUAGE="JavaScript">
cookie_name = "dataCookie";
var YouEntered;
```

```
function putCookie() {
if(document.cookie != document.cookie)
{index = document.cookie.indexOf(cookie_name);}
else
{ index = -1;}
if (index == -1)
{
YouEntered=document.cf.cfd.value;
document.cookie=cookie_name+"="+YouEntered+";
➥expires=Monday, 04-Apr-2010 05:00:00 GMT";
}
}
</SCRIPT>
<FORM NAME="cf">
Enter A Word: <INPUT TYPE="text" NAME="cfd" size="20">
<INPUT TYPE="button" Value="Set to Cookie"
onClick="putCookie()">
</FORM>
```

I know that at this point most people quickly copy and paste the code. When you do, be careful of this line:

```
document.cookie=cookie_name+"="+YouEntered+";
expires=Monday, 04-Apr-2010 05:00:00 GMT";
```

The previous code is on two lines. That's bad. Make sure that it all goes on one line. The width of the page made it break. Fix that when you paste it.

Start from the bottom.

When I talk about a script that deals with an HTML form flag, I like to start with them. So, here goes:

```
<FORM NAME="cf">
Enter A Word: <INPUT TYPE="text" NAME="cfd" size="20">
<INPUT TYPE="button" Value="Set to Cookie"
onClick="putCookie()">
</FORM>
```

The form creates a text box and a button to fire up the function putCookie(). See that? The NAME of the form itself is "cf" and the NAME of the text box is "cfd". Now, when we want to grab what is written in the text box, we create the hierarchy statement document.cf.cfd.value.

Are you still with me? Good. Moving to the script, we'll take it from top to bottom:

```
<SCRIPT LANGUAGE="JavaScript">
```

This starts any JavaScript:

```
cookie_name = "dataCookie";
var YouEntered;
```

The first line names the cookie. A variable `cookie_name` is created, and the name I will call this cookie, `dataCookie`, is assigned.

The second line simply sets a variable named `YouEntered`. We'll assign a value to it later.

Here's the function name that is called for in the form button:

```
function putCookie() {
```

Now we move to the meat of the script:

```
if(document.cookie != document.cookie)
{index = document.cookie.indexOf(cookie_name);}
else
{ index = -1;}
```

The first thing we do is check to see if there even is a cookie. The line `if(document. cookie != document.cookie)` asks if the current cookie is not equal to the data entered by the user.

Writing that question actually saves a step. By asking if something is not equal to something else, I also ask if that something even exists. You see, if it doesn't exist, it cannot be equal. Get it? I'm basically assuring that the cookie is rewritten each time the function is run.

This is an If/Else conditional statement, so here are the items:

If the cookie and the data do not equal, set the cookie with the `cookie_name dataCookie`.

If they do not equal, index is equal to negative one (-1).

Why (-1)? Because JavaScript counts everything starting at zero, so to say to JavaScript that there is actually zero, you need to go one below zero, which is minus one.

Another `If` statement writes to the cookie:

```
if (index == -1)
{
YouEntered=document.cf.cfd.value;
document.cookie=cookie_name+"="+YouEntered+";
```

```
expires=Monday, 04-Apr-2010 05:00:00 GMT";
}
```

Now the variable name `YouEntered` is assigned the value entered into the text box using the `document.cf.cfd.value` hierarchy statement.

Finally, the `document.cookie` is written with the name, what the user entered, and a time for it to expire. I have the "expire" in this script set pretty far into the future. You can set yours to whatever you want; just follow the format shown in the script.

The final curly bracket and `/SCRIPT` round out the script. The cookie is set. Now we have to go get it.

What Does It Look Like?

So, you've set the cookie, but what does it look like? It looks like this:

```
dataCookie
Goodies
~~local~~/D:\HTML Goodies\Working\
029139128323006968326349104029281635*
```

I have the pieces all on separate lines. In the cookie itself, this was all on one line. See the parts? There's the name of the cookie, the word I entered, where the cookie was set (from my hard drive), and then a really long number. That's the number of milliseconds until the expire date. The (*) is the end of the line.

Retrieve the Cookie

Okay, we're set. A cookie has been written, but it's not much good to us unless we can go get it.

I'll show you this in two parts—the JavaScript code that grabs the cookie information and then the HTML/JavaScript that posts it to the page. The following is the code that appeared on the page you went to after setting the cookie.

The Retrieval Script

It looks like this:

```
<SCRIPT LANGUAGE="JavaScript">
cookie_name = "dataCookie";
var YouWrote;
function getName() {
if(document.cookie)
```

```
{
index = document.cookie.indexOf(cookie_name);
if (index != -1)
{
namestart = (document.cookie.indexOf("=", index) + 1);
nameend = document.cookie.indexOf(";", index);
if (nameend == -1) {nameend = document.cookie.length;}
YouWrote = document.cookie.substring(namestart, nameend);
return YouWrote;
}
}
}
YouWrote=getName();
if (YouWrote == "dataCookie")
{YouWrote = "Nothing_Entered"}
</SCRIPT>
```

After hitting the last script, this one should fall together pretty easily. We'll start after the `<SCRIPT LANGUAGE="javascript">` flag:

```
cookie_name = "dataCookie";
var YouWrote;
```

This script assumes that a cookie has been set. In fact, it assumes that many cookies have been set, so the name of the cookie is immediately noted. We are looking for the data found in a cookie named `"dataCookie"`. A variable, `YouWrote`, is also created. Later, it will be assigned the value from the cookie. You'll then use `YouWrote` to represent the cookie's data:

```
function getName() {
```

The function is called `getName()`.

```
if(document.cookie)
{
index = document.cookie.indexOf(cookie_name);
```

If no cookie exists, the index should be the one in `dataCookie`; but we know one exists.

```
if (index != -1)
{
namestart = (document.cookie.indexOf("=", index) + 1);
nameend = document.cookie.indexOf(";", index);
if (nameend == -1) {nameend = document.cookie.length;}
YouWrote = document.cookie.substring(namestart, nameend);
return YouWrote;
```

```
    }
  }
}
```

As you saw previously, it is the second piece of information in the cookie we're interested in. This code grabs a substring of the cookie represented by the second item. It then assigns that value to YouWrote and returns it to the script:

```
YouWrote=getName();
```

Every function must have a trigger to make it work. Here's the one that fires up getName(), assigning its output to YouWrote:

```
if (YouWrote == "dataCookie")
{YouWrote = "Nothing_Entered"}
```

This little blip of code is used if nothing is entered. When you submit nothing (no data) to the cookie, the name of the cookie is returned by the function. This says that if the YouWrote equals dataCookie, the name of the cookie, the value assigned should be "Nothing_Entered". It just looks a little cleaner.

Putting the Cookie on the Page

It's a fairly simple process from this point on. You have a variable, YouWrote, that represents the value of the cookie. Just use that variable name to post the data to the page through document.write commands. This is how I did it on the secondary page in this tutorial:

```
<SCRIPT LANGUAGE="javascript">
document.write("You Entered " +YouWrote+ ".");
</SCRIPT>
<SCRIPT LANGUAGE="javascript">
document.write("<FORM>")
document.write("You Entered:")
document.write("<INPUT TYPE=text SIZE=30 VALUE=" +YouWrote+ ">");
document.write("</FORM>")
</SCRIPT>
```

The first simply prints it to the page, and the second puts it into a text box. Note the code that creates the text box requires the <FORM> flags, too.

More Than One Cookie

The code you got here is pretty much copy-and-paste easy to install. But let's say that you want to set multiple cookies. You'll need to remember that the two scripts you got here are links. The first sets the cookie, and the second retrieves it. So any changes you make to one script, you'll need to make to the other.

First and foremost, you'll need to set a new cookie name, and then new variable names to represent the data. Please note that those variable names appear throughout the script, so make sure that you get them all. I do it with my text editor's Replace All function.

If you grab the cookie the way I did, using a form, you'll need to make sure that the form element's NAMEs are correctly represented in the script's hierarchy statements.

Don't sweat it. It's a little work, but you'll get it down soon enough. Just remember to keep a backup of the original working scripts. I wasted over an hour this time around by editing the original. That's what I get for writing a JavaScript book...

Cookie Counter

I wrote two cookie tutorials one right after the other. Both were written in response to Goodies reader requests. In the first tutorial, I put together a script that would place and retrieve a cookie. It's the preceding one. You'll want to read it first if you haven't already.

In this tutorial, I'm going to use a cookie to count the number of times a computer has been to your site. The purpose of the script is to place the cookie and retrieve it, adding one each time it visits.

Now, to be fair, this counter will only work as long as the person allows the cookie to stay put. The moment he goes into the guts of his browser directory and erases the cookie, the count is dead.

Also, before you start placing cookies all over the Net, please take the time to read my cookies reference piece. Many people don't want you placing cookies. You need to decide if this counter is worth the hassle it might bring you.

That said, we'll move on.

 You can find this tutorial, and all of its examples, online at `http://www.htmlgoodies.com/ beyond/cookiecount.html.`

 You can download just the examples at `http://www.htmlgoodies.com/wpg/.`

The Effect

The following script has three parents: me, a gentleman named Mac, who submitted something similar to me, and a JavaScript cookies help site that also offered something similar. I took parts from each, found an easier method of setting the "expires" date, and this is what I came up with.

Figure 7.3 shows what the script produces online. I took the screen capture right from the tutorial page.

Figure 7.3
...and I'll be back a third time.

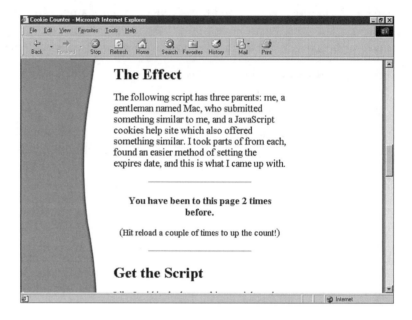

Get the Script

Like I said in the last cookie tutorial, setting these things can be rough. Luckily, this one is a simple copy and paste and you're done. If you're already setting a cookie called Counter_Cookie, that could get in the way, so be careful with naming.

Here's the code. It's fully functional just as you see it:

```
<SCRIPT LANGUAGE="JavaScript">
<!-- Hide script
cookie_name = "Counter_Cookie";
function doCookie() {
if(document.cookie)
{index = document.cookie.indexOf(cookie_name);}
else
{index = -1;}
var expires = "Monday, 04-Apr-2010 05:00:00 GMT"
if (index == -1)
{document.cookie=cookie_name+"=1; expires=" + expires;}
else
{
countbegin = (document.cookie.indexOf("=", index) + 1);
```

```
countend = document.cookie.indexOf(";", index);
if (countend == -1) {
countend = document.cookie.length;
}
count = eval(document.cookie.substring(countbegin,
➥countend)) + 1;
document.cookie=cookie_name+"="+count+"; expires=" + expires;
}
}
function gettimes() {
if(document.cookie) {
index = document.cookie.indexOf(cookie_name);
if (index != -1) {
countbegin = (document.cookie.indexOf("=", index) + 1);
countend = document.cookie.indexOf(";", index);
if (countend == -1) {
countend = document.cookie.length;
}
count = document.cookie.substring(countbegin, countend);
if (count == 1) {
return (count+" time");
} else {
return (count+" times");
}
}
}
return ("0 times");
}
// done hiding script -->
</SCRIPT>
<body onLoad="doCookie()">
<center>
<SCRIPT LANGUAGE="javascript">
document.write("<b>You have been to my site
➥"+gettimes()+" before.</b>");
</SCRIPT>
</center>
```

Explaining the Script

Because this is, for the most part, a straight copy and paste (you can get the script online), let me simply offer the script again in text form and explain what each section does. If you've read the other cookie tutorial, this should make quick sense.

187

Cookie Count Script Explanation

All explanation appears in bold text:

```
<SCRIPT LANGUAGE="JavaScript">
<!-- Hide script
//This starts the script then hides it from lesser browsers.
cookie_name = "Counter_Cookie";
//The cookie name is set as Counter_Cookie. If you're going
//to put this onto other pages to count them, change this
//with a new name.
function doCookie() {
if(document.cookie)
{index = document.cookie.indexOf(cookie_name);}
//Is there a cookie named Counter_Cookie? If so, use that.
else
{index = -1;}
//If there isn't, set the index to minus one (-1).
var expires = "Monday, 04-Apr-2010 05:00:00 GMT"
//A variable is set up to represent the "expires" date.
if (index == -1)
{document.cookie=cookie_name+"=1; expires=" + expires;}
//If the index was set to minus one, then set the cookie
//with the name Counter_Cookie, a number 1, then the
//expires date.
else
{
countbegin = (document.cookie.indexOf("=", index) + 1);
countend = document.cookie.indexOf(";", index);
if (countend == -1) {
countend = document.cookie.length;
}
count = eval(document.cookie.substring(countbegin, countend))
➥+ 1;
document.cookie=cookie_name+"="+count+"; expires=" + expires;
}
}
//If not, then take the number in the cookie already and
//add one. Then rewrite the cookie with the new number.
function gettimes() {
//This starts the second function that gets the
//value in the cookie and assigns it to a variable name.
if(document.cookie) {
index = document.cookie.indexOf(cookie_name);
```

```
if (index != -1) {
countbegin = (document.cookie.indexOf("=", index) + 1);
countend = document.cookie.indexOf(";", index);
//Grab the second piece of information in the cookie,
//the number (see the +1?).
if (countend == -1) {
countend = document.cookie.length;
}
count = document.cookie.substring(countbegin, countend);
if (count == 1) {
return (count+" time");
} else {
return (count+" times");
//If the count is one, then return the singular "time."
//If the count is more, return the plural "times."
}
}
}
return ("0 times");
//If the number is 0, then return "0 times."
}
// done hiding script -->
</SCRIPT>
//End the script.
<body onLoad="doCookie()">
//An onLoad Event Handler fires the function to place the cookie.
<center>
<SCRIPT LANGUAGE="javascript">
document.write("<b>You have been to my site "+gettimes()+"
➥before.</b>");
</SCRIPT>
</center>
//Another script uses a document.write statement to place
//the output of the gettimes() function on the page.
```

More Than One

If you intend to use the counter script on multiple pages, keep in mind that you'll need to assign a new cookie name for each page. If you don't, all the pages containing the script will affect the same cookie and the count will be a total of all the pages on your site that the person has visited rather than a count of that one page. Now, maybe you want that because it would certainly kick the number up faster...

But if you're a good, decent, honorable human being (and I know you are) and want your counts to reflect true visitation numbers, make sure that you change the name of the cookie every time you place this script on a page. You only have to change it once, in the third line of the script.

Disabling Mouse Clicks

Okay, okay, okay, I give! I'll post a short tutorial on stopping people from clicking on your page!

At least once a day, a question is asked about how to disable someone's right- or left-click mouse button. The reasoning behind it is that it will somehow stop prying eyes from seeing your code or stop sticky fingers from stealing your images.

I guess there's some validity in the right-click reasoning in that someone new to the game might be put off when they are told, "No Right Clicking!" However, let me point out a couple of things before you begin posting these scripts on every page, thinking it's a lock and key for your valuables.

A Web-Head who knows what he is doing can get your code or your images no matter what you put in place. I have had two people write and tell me that they have found a way to stop me from stealing their images. A few minutes later, I sent them their images over email. I'm not bragging: I'm simply telling you the truth. If your page or your images display on my computer, I can get them. It just isn't that hard.

 You can find this tutorial, and all of its examples, online at `http://www.htmlgoodies.com/beyond/noclick.html.`

 You can download just the examples at `http://www.htmlgoodies.com/wpg/.`

This only works in Internet Explorer. Netscape users can happily right-click you to death.

So, if you want to use these as a first line of defense, great. Just know that they are not foolproof, nor do they affect everyone. That said, we'll start with the right.

No Right Click

It's all done through the magic of JavaScript. The No Right Click script looks like this:

```
<SCRIPT LANGUAGE="javascript">
function click() {
if (event.button==2) {
alert('Sorry, this function is disabled.')
}
}
```

```
document.onMouseDown=click
</SCRIPT>
```

As you might have guessed, the `event.button` is the real trigger. The number 2 simply represents the right button. The alert button comes into play when the right button is clicked, negating the click altogether. Do you want to see it? Figure 7.4 has the proof of the alert box.

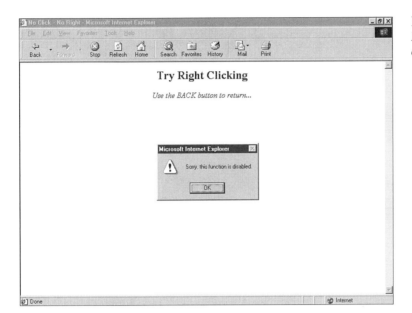

Figure 7.4
No right-clicking by order of Field Marshall Burns.

No Left Click

You can probably guess at how this one is done, but here's the script:

```
<SCRIPT LANGUAGE="javascript">
function click() {
if (event.button==1) {
alert('No clicking!')
}
}
document.onMouseDown=click
</SCRIPT>
```

New let's take a look at it. Figure 7.5 shows it all.

Figure 7.5
No left-clicking...or else!
(No one expects the
Spanish Inquisition!)

No Clicking at All!

That means you! If you want to completely disable someone's mouse, try altering either script so that the alert will display no matter what button is pushed. It looks like this:

```
<SCRIPT LANGUAGE="javascript">
function click() {
if (event.button==1 || event.button==2) {
alert('No clicking!')
}
}
document.onMouseDown=click
</SCRIPT>
```

Want to go somewhere where you can't click at all? Enjoy Figure 7.6.

By themselves, the scripts are not overly useful, but they might be helpful for a larger effect you're trying to achieve.

Figure 7.6
The Land of no clicks. (A Quinn-Martin Production)

Minimize and Maximize Buttons

This is an effect I have been using for a short while on some other sites I've worked on, and I thought it might make a nice tutorial. I'm really sorry to say that at the time of this tutorial (7/28/00—Kathie Lee's last day with Regis), it only works on Netscape Navigator 4.0 and above.

 You can find this tutorial, and all of its examples, online at `http://www.htmlgoodies.com/beyond/minmax.html`.

 You can download just the examples at `http://www.htmlgoodies.com/wpg/`.

I mainly use the effect when I open smaller windows, in order to allow the user to see one piece of code while reading over text in the larger, parent window. Often I'll have two extra windows apart from the parent, and these commands will allow the user to minimize and maximize the windows.

Mind you, I only offer the code on pages that will display on Navigator 4.0 and above. I get that effect by using an internal browser test script. Remember that from Chapter 4, "What About the Page's Design"?

Okay, that's enough talking. Let's see it. Please understand that you must be running Netscape Navigator 4 or better to see it. After you click Minimize, wait one moment. Not only will the screen get smaller, it'll jump to the bottom right portion of the screen. It's really a neat effect. (See Figures 7.7 and 7.8.)

Figure 7.7
Full sized screen. I click on the text, Minimize, and...

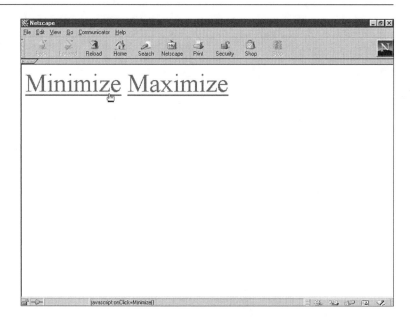

Figure 7.8
Ba Da Bing!

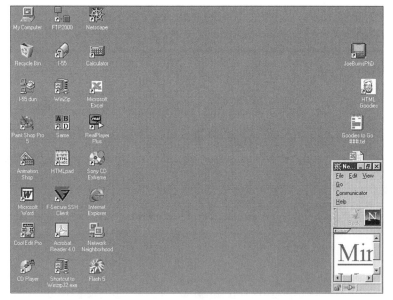

The Code

Here's the code that makes it big and makes it small:

```
<SCRIPT LANGUAGE="JavaScript">
function Minimize()
{
window.innerWidth = 100;
window.innerHeight = 100;
window.screenX = screen.width;
window.screenY = screen.height;
alwaysLowered = true;
}
function Maximize()
{
window.innerWidth = screen.width;
window.innerHeight = screen.height;
window.screenX = 0;
window.screenY = 0;
alwaysLowered = false;
}
</SCRIPT>
<A HREF="javascript:onClick=Minimize()">Minimize</A>
<A HREF="javascript:onClick=Maximize()">Maximize</A>
```

Here's What's Happening

You'll notice that I have actually set up two functions—one that maximizes and one that minimizes. If you understand one, you'll certainly be able to pick apart the other. Let's look at the first one.

There are other methods of getting the same resize effect, but the first time I saw this done, the author used the `innerWidth` and `innerHeight` commands, so I kept it that way. Those two commands deal with the inner browser window measurements in pixels. Notice that I have the window set to measure 100 by 100 pixels.

The next two lines set a point so that the `alwaysLowered` command will be able to lower and move the window to the bottom right of the screen. `Minimize` sets X and Y to the full screen size, and `Maximize` sets it to the zero points so that the maximized screen goes all the way up to the left corner.

The triggers for the events are JavaScript links:

```
<A HREF="javascript:onClick=Minimize()">Minimize</A>
```

Click on a link, and one function or the other is triggered. Your screen will minimize or maximize. Because the script is set up to read and work with whatever screen setting you or your users have set up, just copy, paste, and you're good to go.

This isn't an effect you'll want to use a great deal. I use it only sparingly myself, but I have used it.

When you do incorporate it into a page, be sure that you put the links that create the effect in the upper left corner. That way, they will be visible even when the screen minimizes and jumps down to the lower right corner.

Refresh the Page

I started to get email asking for this effect right around the time Internet stocks took off. People wrote asking how the stock sites got their pages to reload all by themselves.

The answer is pretty easy, so I usually just wrote and answered in the email. While going through my notebook of possible topics, this one came up as one that is asked a fair amount of the time, so I thought I'd write up a quick tutorial.

 You can find this tutorial, and all of its examples, online at `http://www.htmlgoodies.com/tutors/refresh.html`.

 You can download just the examples at `http://www.htmlgoodies.com/wpg/`.

The trick to reloading the page is to force the browser to not look into the cache, but rather to again make a connection to the Web and bring up the document from the server. Most people know it can be done by hand by holding the shift key and clicking the Refresh (on IE) or Reload (on Navigator) buttons. If you didn't know, now you do.

That's a proven method, but it's not exactly very pretty to have text asking the user to hold and click. You want your site to do the trick either by itself or by offering a method in which users simply click and the browser does it for them.

Next I have two methods. One will reload every so many seconds on its own, and the other will reload when the user asks for it.

Reload All by Itself

This one's nice and easy. I'll give you the code. Copy and paste it into the document you want to reload. Once it's in there, change the number of seconds you want the page to wait before starting the reloading process. This code goes in between the HEAD flags:

```
<META HTTP-EQUIV="refresh" CONTENT="15">
```

Right now, the command is set to reload every 15 seconds. I checked a couple of online sites, and they were all set about the same. I found that the sites displaying stock information were set to around five minutes or 300 seconds.

I don't have a refresh on this page because the darn thing would just keep refreshing and there's nothing on this page that will update.

Reload from a User's Click

I've seen this done a number of ways, but this is my favorite because it, again, forces the browser to load from the server. It is true that pages can become cached if they are reloaded a great many times, but I have had pretty good success with this. Try it.

Click to Refresh the Page

Here's the code:

```
<A HREF="javascript:history.go(0)">Click to refresh the page</A>
```

Rather than using a refresh command, I like to go to the history of the page and set it to 0. The 0 is the current page because in JavaScript, lists (arrays) are numbered starting with zero. Here's the same effect in button code:

```
<FORM>
<INPUT TYPE="button" onClick="history.go(0)" VALUE="Refresh">
</FORM>
```

Use the Full URL?

Again, it's possible that a page using the methods shown previously can get cached and can stop reloading from the server. A Webmaster friend told me that if you simply set up a link to the current page but use the entire URL, the page would always reload from the server because the request starts at the domain. For example, the full URL of this tutorial's online page is http://www.htmlgoodies.com/tutors/refresh.html.

If you use that full URL in each of the preceding elements, you'll lessen the chance that the page will cache. Thus, the Meta Refresh would become

```
<META HTTP-EQUIV="refresh" CONTENT="5;
URL=http://www.htmlgoodies.com/tutors/refresh.html">
```

You would then change out the preceding JavaScript formats to simply go to the URL rather than looking at the history file. In fact, you could lose the JavaScript altogether and just make a simple A HREF link right to the current page. The trick is to use the full URL address so that the process starts at the very beginning.

Again, the effect is the same as you'll get with the previous code. It just lowers the chance of the page getting stuck in cache.

It's short, sweet, and simple. The effect is useful if done correctly. Two methods of using the effect incorrectly are refreshing so that a counter increases and refreshing so that a new banner ad displays. You don't want to refresh your page unless there's a very good reason. Programs are out there that update banners without refreshing the entire page. The use of the refresh to display new counter numbers is just silly.

And yes, I have seen both usages, or I wouldn't have thought to bring them up.

HTA Files

I get letters all the time asking if I would offer the tutorials found on the HTML Goodies site as downloads. That way, the tutorials could be viewed without being logged on. My answer is usually "no," simply because of copyright concerns.

Well, one day I get a letter from a reader who suggested that if I ever did offer my tutorials for downloading, HTA format might be the way to do it. I didn't know what HTA format was, so I checked into it.

 You can find this tutorial, and all of its examples, online at `http://www.htmlgoodies.com/beyond/hta.html.`

 You can download just the examples at `http://www.htmlgoodies.com/wpg/.`

The Basic Concept

HTA stands for *HTML Application*. It's a concept from the research kitchens of Microsoft and works with all computers running Explorer browsers 5.0 and above. Notice that I said "running" MSIE 5.0. This HTA does not work within the browser; rather, HTA allows you to create a downloadable file that takes with it all the information regarding how it will display and be rendered.

HTA understands everything the browser understands including HTML and CSS code. Microsoft described an HTA as running much like an .exe file. The browser will ask if you'd like to download an HTA just like any other .exe file. HTAs will run from your system, so they are not bound by security or privacy concerns found on the Internet. Of course, one can see multiple benefits and concerns in such a file because after the file is downloaded and run, it is seen as a trusted program and has access to the system it is sitting on.

That said, let's look into an HTA.

The HTA File

When I first began reading about HTAs, I kept getting that it was easy to create them. All you need to do is to take any HTML (or text) file and give it the .hta extension. This is true, but it's not really doing the format justice. As I said before, where the real fire comes in is being able to configure the display of the file.

I added this text in the HEAD section of an HTML document:

```
<HTA:APPLICATION
border="thin"
borderStyle="normal"
caption="yes"
icon="http://www.htmlgoodies.com/favicon.ico"
maximizeButton="yes"
minimizeButton="yes"
showInTaskbar="no"
windowState="maximize"
innerBorder="yes"
navigable="yes"
scroll="auto"
scrollFlat="yes" />
```

That's the flag/attribute code I've set up to alter the window that will contain the display of the HTA.

Now, go ahead and download the HTA file by going to http://www.htmlgoodies.com/beyond/hta.html. When you attempt to download, you'll get the familiar box asking if you'd like to download the file. Say yes and download it where you can quickly find it.

After you've got it, go the file on your hard drive. The icon will be the little flying Windows logo. Click on it and up will come the viewer with this tutorial displayed just as I suggested in the preceding code. After you've looked, come back and we'll look into what each of the elements does.

Figure 7.9 shows my computer after I have downloaded the file "example.hta." I opened the file by clicking on it from my computer's hard drive. What popped up is the HTA file.

The Flag and Properties

Well, how did it look? My guess is that it looked just like this without all the orange swoosh and image stuff. That was on purpose. I didn't see a need to add it all into the code. My guess is that all you really wanted was the text, so that's all I gave. Did you also get the little HG icon in the upper left corner? If not, you must not have been attached to the Web when you viewed the HTA file. I set the file so that it would go out on the Web and grab that icon when displayed.

Figure 7.9
What the HTA? Notice the icon in the upper left corner.

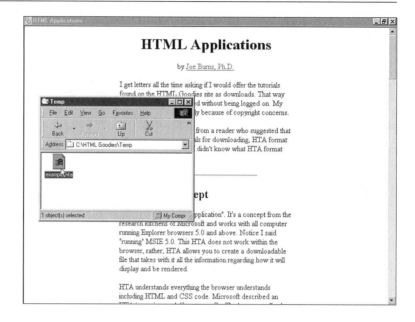

Okay, let's tear it apart.

Again, the HTA:APPLICATION flag goes in between the HEAD flags. Although it might not look like it up previously, the flag does require a close flag. That means you can use </HTA:APPLICATION> to close up the flag if you'd like. I used a bit of shorthand suggested by the Microsoft pages.

Notice that I have a space and then a slash just before the >. That's an easy way to say "end." You'll see that format being used a great deal in XML if you start getting into the language.

Where the flag really comes alive are all the properties (properties of the attribute "application") you can play with. I've used just about every one previously that will alter the look of the display. Notice how I have them listed—one after another and at least one space between each. I have a line break. It's the same thing, but with no commas. Put your flag together just the same way you see mine earlier.

Here are the properties and what they do:

- **border** sets the border format.
  Options: thin, dialog, none, thick.

- **borderStyle** further defines the border.
  Options: complex, normal, raised, static, sunken.

- **caption** denotes a title bar or not.
  Options: yes, no.

- **icon** is the path to an icon that will display in the title bar, not on the hard drive. Options: The icon must be 32×32 "ico" format. I found it works pretty well if you have a favicon.ico on your system to attach to that. That's what I did previously.

- **maximizeButton** is the max button in the title bar. Options: yes, no.

- **minimizeButton** is the min button in the title bar. Options: yes, no.

- **showInTaskbar** tells if the application will display in the taskbar. Options: yes, no.

- **windowState** is how the window will display. Options: normal, minimize, maximize.

- **innerBorder** denotes whether you'll have one or not. Options: yes, no.

- **navigable** suggests whether linked pages will display in the HTA window or not. Options: yes, no.

- **scroll** denotes a scrollbar. Options: yes, no, auto.

- **scrollFlat** denotes whether the scrollbar will be 3D or not. Options: yes, no.

There are a few other properties, and if you'd like to get into them, feel free. The only properties I covered here are those that deal with the display, the design, of the HTA.

For some further reading, try the MSIE Web Workshop page at
http://msdn.microsoft.com/library/default.asp?url=/workshop/author/hta/overview/htaoverview.asp.

I think it's a good thing to use if you're going to offer downloads and want those pages to work the same way as the Web site.

Keystroke Captures

Here's a great trick that I stumbled across while surfing for a completely different topic. One of the things you're looking for when creating a Web site is interaction. You want your Web pages to play with the people reading and typing to them.

To that end, now and again you might want to know when someone presses a specific key. The first example that comes to mind is any kind of game you might want to create. Using this JavaScript, you can set up the board so that certain keyboard strokes do certain things. You might also want to set this up with a form. Let's say that you have a form element that cannot contain the tilde character. With this script, you can set it up so that when the user presses tilde, bang. An alert pops up and warns against it.

 You can find this tutorial, and all of its examples, online at `http://www.htmlgoodies.com/beyond/keycapture.html`.

 You can download just the examples at `http://www.htmlgoodies.com/wpg/`.

The example I ran into simply denoted if numbers were pushed. When I began to really play with the script, it occurred to me that even though all ASCII characters are equal in terms of a numeric element, they are not equal on the keyboard. The script had to deal with both keys stroked while in lowercase and keys stroked while in uppercase. Furthermore, and you could probably see this coming, there was no one script that worked in both Netscape and Internet Explorer.

No kidding, huh? Well, after cursing and yelling a good bit, this is what I came up with. To see the script in action, dig Figure 7.10.

Figure 7.10
I pushed the key to get a percentage sign...obviously.

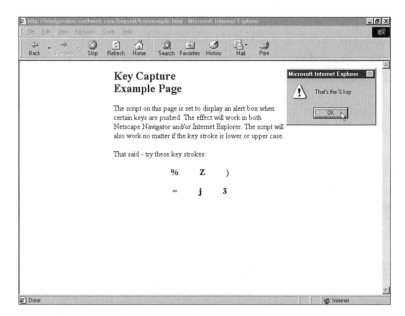

The Script

It looks like this:

```
<HEAD>
<SCRIPT LANGUAGE="JavaScript1.2">
<!--
```

```
function NNKeyCap(thisOne)
{
 if (thisOne.modifiers & Event.SHIFT_MASK)
{
 if (thisOne.which == 37)
 {alert('That\'s the % key')};
 if (thisOne.which == 90)
 {alert('That\'s the Z key')};
 if (thisOne.which == 41)
 {alert('That\'s the ) key')};
}
 if (thisOne.which == 61)
 {alert('That\'s the = key')};
 if (thisOne.which == 106)
 {alert('That\'s the j key')};
 if (thisOne.which == 51)
 {alert('That\'s the 3 key')};
}
function IEKeyCap()
{
if (window.event.shiftKey)
{
 if (window.event.keyCode == 37)
 {alert('That\'s the % key')};
 if (window.event.keyCode == 90)
 {alert('That\'s the Z key')};
 if (window.event.keyCode == 41)
 {alert('That\'s the ) key')};
}
 if (window.event.keyCode == 61)
 {alert('That\'s the = key')};
 if (window.event.keyCode == 106)
 {alert('That\'s the j key')};
 if (window.event.keyCode == 51)
 {alert('That\'s the 3 key')};
}
if (navigator.appName == 'Netscape') {
window.captureEvents(Event.KEYPRESS);
window.onKeyPress = NNKeyCap;
}
//-->
</SCRIPT>
</HEAD>
<BODY onKeyPress="IEKeyCap()">
```

The Netscape Portion

I've attempted to label the elements of the script well enough so that you can more easily pick out what each part does. We'll start with the top third of the script first. It deals with Netscape browsers:

```
function NNKeyCap(thisOne)
{
 if (thisOne.modifiers & Event.SHIFT_MASK)
{
 if (thisOne.which == 37)
 {alert('That\'s the % key')};
 if (thisOne.which == 90)
 {alert('That\'s the Z key')};
 if (thisOne.which == 41)
 {alert('That\'s the ) key')};
}
 if (thisOne.which == 61)
 {alert('That\'s the = key')};
 if (thisOne.which == 106)
 {alert('That\'s the j key')};
 if (thisOne.which == 51)
 {alert('That\'s the 3 key')};
}
```

It's a fairly straightforward function named NNKeyCap(). The top part asks if the Shift key is held down. That's this line:

```
 if (thisOne.modifiers & Event.SHIFT_MASK)
```

If it is held down, these six lines come into play:

```
{
 if (thisOne.which == 37)
 {alert('That\'s the % key')};
 if (thisOne.which == 90)
 {alert('That\'s the Z key')};
 if (thisOne.which == 41)
 {alert('That\'s the ) key')};
}
```

Notice that the function will be passed a number upon the keystroke. That number is set in these three lines. 37 represents the % character, 90 represents the Z character, and 41 represents the) character. These characters are created by holding down the Shift key.

Each of the `if` statements then have what should happen within the curly brackets. In this case, I have a simple alert command. If you want to use this script and have something more amazing, you would put the code inside the curly brackets following each keystroke identifier.

But what if the Shift key is not pressed?

The script is set up so that if the Shift key is not pressed, the next set of conditions come into play:

```
if (thisOne.which == 61)
{alert('That\'s the = key')};
if (thisOne.which == 106)
{alert('That\'s the j key')};
if (thisOne.which == 51)
{alert('That\'s the 3 key')};
}
```

The format is exactly the same, except the numbers and letters have been changed. Each of the three keys noted here do not require that the Shift key be pressed.

WAIT!

How do you know what number represents what key? I'll get to that. Stay tuned, but now we'll go back to the script…

The function `NNKeyCap()` is fired using this little blip of code at the end of the script:

```
if (navigator.appName == 'Netscape') {
window.captureEvents(Event.KEYPRESS);
window.onKeyPress = NNKeyCap;
```

I stuck it at the end because of the way the script works. Basically the `NNKeyCap()` function is loaded into RAM before any of the keys can be stroked so it will work straight away. It seems a little backward, but that's the reasoning.

The MSIE Portion

The MSIE portion of the script works almost exactly the same way. Some of the names have been changed because of a difference in jargon, plus the function is now triggered in the `BODY` flag. Look at the full script again. You'll see the `onKeyPress` in the `BODY` flag. It's important that you have that.

The IE portion looks like this:

```
function IEKeyCap()
{
if (window.event.ShiftKey)
{
 if (window.event.keyCode == 37)
 {alert('That\'s the % key')};
 if (window.event.keyCode == 90)
 {alert('That\'s the Z key')};
 if (window.event.keyCode == 41)
 {alert('That\'s the ) key')};
}
 if (window.event.keyCode == 61)
 {alert('That\'s the = key')};
 if (window.event.keyCode == 106)
 {alert('That\'s the j key')};
 if (window.event.keyCode == 51)
 {alert('That\'s the 3 key')};
}
```

That should look rather familiar. The first section checks to see if the Shift key is pressed and if so, these specific numbers are "listened" for. If the Shift key is not pressed, the next little blip of code comes into play.

Altering the Script

The script is written so that altering it is very easy without disrupting the remainder of the text.

To pick a new character for the script to react to, you simply enter the new number in the correct place—in both sections. I mean, you want this to work on both browsers right?

I have placed the alerts inside curly brackets. The text I have in there is very small, but as any JavaScript programmer knows, you can spread those brackets very wide apart and put just about any event or script in there. The script is quite malleable on purpose.

What About the Numbers?

The numbers are the ACSII numbers that represent the character. There are 128 in all. Here's a link to a full list: http://www.jimprice.com/ascii-0-127.gif.

What I have listed here are the numbers you will be most interested in. These are the keys on your computer keyboard. Just change out the number shown with the number in the script, and that key becomes active in the script. Here are the correlations:

09 = Tab	11 = Home	13 = Enter
32 = Space	33 = !	34 = "
35 = #	36 = $	37 = %
38 = &	39 = '	40 = (
41 =)	42 = *	43 = +
44 = ,	45 = -	46 = .
47 = /	48 = 0	49 = 1
50 = 2	51 = 3	52 = 4
53 = 5	54 = 6	55 = 7
56 = 8	57 = 9	58 = :
59 = ;	60 = <	61 = =
62 = >	63 = ?	64 = @
65 = A	66 = B	67 = C
68 = D	69 = E	70 = F
71 = G	72 = H	73 = I
74 = J	75 = K	76 = L
77 = M	78 = N	79 = O
80 = P	81 = Q	82 = R
83 = S	84 = T	85 = U
86 = V	87 = W	88 = X
89 = Y	90 = Z	91 = [
92 = \	93 =]	94 = ^
95 = -	96 = `	97 = a
98 = b	99 = c	100 = d
101 = e	102 = f	103 = g
104 = h	105 = i	106 = j
107 = k	108 = l	109 = m
110 = n	111 = o	112 = p
113 = q	114 = r	115 = s
116 = t	117 = u	118 = v
119 = w	120 = x	121 = y
122 = z	123 = {	124 =	
125 = }	126 = ~	

Chapter 8

They'll Never See These, But They'll Thank You for Them

There are also many things you can do for your viewers behind the scenes. They will never know you put these here. But in the end, the pages will run smoother, the users will be more at ease on your site, and they'll never know. These tips include

- Do Not Cache a Page
- Server Response Codes
- Alternative Printing
- Make Your Own PDF Pages
- OnError Event Handler
- Flash Plug-in Test Page
- XHTML

Do Not Cache a Page

I get letters now and again asking how to make it so that when a page is loaded into a browser, that page will not be loaded into the browser's cache. Someone would want to do this for a few different reasons. First, if the page contains information that will be readily updated through a refresh command of some sort, you don't want a page in cache to thwart the process. You want the page to be reloaded from the server each time.

Another big concern is when someone is filling out forms. You really don't want the pages cached because if they are, credit card numbers, addresses, and all kinds of stuff can be gathered from the cached page.

 You can find this tutorial online at `http://www.htmlgoodies.com/beyond/nocache.html`.

When people talk about not caching a page, talk of this command usually comes up:

```
<META HTTP-EQUIV="Pragma" CONTENT="no-cache">
```

The old statement was always plop that between your HEAD commands and you're good to go. There's no cache! Well, that's just not the case. There are bugs in both Netscape Navigator (NN) and Internet Explorer (IE).

So, if you're really interested in not caching a page, read on.

IE First

The preceding Pragma, or directing, statement sometimes fails in IE because of the way IE caches files. A 64KB buffer must be filled before a page is cached in IE. The problem is that the vast majority of the pages using the Pragma statement put it between the HEAD flags.

The HEAD loads and the Pragma comes into play. The browser gets the go aHEAD to not cache the page; however, there is not yet a page to not cache. How's that for backward logic? Because the page hasn't filled the 64KB buffer, there's no page, so the Pragma is ignored. Thus, the page is cached.

The solution is to play to the buffer. If you're really serious about the Pragma working, place another set of HEAD flags at the bottom of the document, before the end HTML flag, and re-enter the Pragma. This is a suggestion straight from Microsoft Support. The page would look like this:

```
<HTML>
<HEAD>
<TITLE>---</TITLE>
<META HTTP-EQUIV="Pragma" CONTENT="no-cache">
</HEAD>
<BODY>
```

Text in the browser window looks like this:

```
</BODY>
<HEAD>
<META HTTP-EQUIV="Pragma" CONTENT="no-cache">
```

```
</HEAD>
</HTML>
```

This way, the Pragma is pretty sure to be read when the buffer is filled.

Pragma Doesn't Work in IE 5

It was news to me too. In order to assure a non-cache, you'll need to add another metatag:

```
<META HTTP-EQUIV="Expires" CONTENT="-1">
```

That sets an immediate expiration on the file. Thus, it dies the moment is it born. Place it on your page in the same manner as previously. Because you still have the 64KB buffer problem to worry about, I would place it in both HEAD flag sections. Better to be safe than sorry. It should look like this:

```
<HTML>
<HEAD>
<TITLE>---</TITLE>
<META HTTP-EQUIV="Pragma" CONTENT="no-cache">
<META HTTP-EQUIV="Expires" CONTENT="-1">
</HEAD>
<BODY>
```

Text in the browser window looks like this:

```
</BODY>
<HEAD>
<META HTTP-EQUIV="Pragma" CONTENT="no-cache">
<META HTTP-EQUIV="Expires" CONTENT="-1">
</HEAD>
</HTML>
```

ASP Pages Use This

If you write in ASP and want the same non-cache effect, here's the headerheader information.

```
<% Response.CacheControl = "no-cache" %>>
<% Response.Addheaderheader "Pragma", "no-cache" %>
<% Response.Expires = -1 %>
```

I didn't read anything about placing it a second time, but better safe than sorry.

211

Navigator Next

Netscape Navigator recognizes a bug when using the Pragma in secure server situations. The site states that even if the Pragma command is used, as long as the browser is never closed, the Back button will enable someone to see the information entered.

Netscape suggests that people shut down the browser after entering to the screen so that the Back button doesn't have a history to scroll through.

In addition, Netscape suggests the following JavaScript be used in the BODY flag of all pages that should not be cached:

```
onLoad="if ('Navigator' == navigator.appName)
document.forms[0].reset();"
```

All of my readings got in to the concept of Pragma in both secure and non-secure settings. I guess there's some reason to it, but I'm a fan of not taking chances. If you want a page to not cache, put these statements on it. But keep in mind, there might very well still be a hole no one has found yet.

Server Response Codes

Ah, you received a dreaded error message. You were surfing along just fine when all of a sudden you get that horrible white screen with the big number up in the corner.

Most of you know the 404 Error. That means the server can't find the page you're looking for. I hate that one. It always seems to pop up when I'm using a search engine trying to find a specific topic. Just when I find a page that looks perfect—boom, the 404 Error appears. Ugh!

 You can find this tutorial online at `http://www.htmlgoodies.com/tutors/src.html`.

What you might not know is that there are errors other than the 404. Oh, yeah! There's a whole run of fun little error messages that can plague you into submission. As a surfer, you're probably most familiar with the 400 and 500 level errors. Those are the most common ones to pop up in a browser window.

The 404, and all of its numeric partners, are what are known as Server Response Codes (SRC). They're created when the server itself sends back a message that all is okay or that all has gone wrong. Most of these you'll never see because they act silently. That means, the response is given that all is okay and the process continues without your ever seeing the response given. Those SRCs are numbers found mostly within 100 through 399. Then there are those that you get to see. Those you find mostly within the 400 to 599 range.

In the following descriptions, I'm going to say that the header was the reason for the error again and again. So what's a header?

Headers

This has nothing to do with the HTML <HEAD> flags. I'm talking about something different here. I'm talking about headers. A header is text that is used to transfer information between clients and servers. You will never see the headers unless you get deeper into programming on the server itself. They're created by the machines that move information around on the Web. There are basically four types of headers:

- General—This is information related to the client, the server, or the protocol (like HTTP or FTP).
- Entity—This is information about the actual data being transferred.
- Request—This sets standards regarding acceptable formats and parameters.
- Response—This contains information about the server sending the response.

Every time a server is contacted to by a user, a "handshake" occurs. This is where the two machines "talk" to each other, make sure that they can connect, and then create the transfer you are asking for. These headers are used to provide all the information required to have a successful handshake.

The following codes are created as a result of that handshake.

The Server Response Codes (SRCs)

Here's how it all breaks down. Man, you'll impress your friends at your next cocktail party by knowing all these.

100-199 Codes

SRCs provide confirmation that a request was received and is being processed. These are silent.

- 100—This is good. The request was completed and the process can move along.
- 101—Request to switch protocols (like from HTTP to FTP) was accepted.

200-299 Codes

SRCs report that requests were performed successfully. These are silent.

- 200—It simply means that all is okay. What the client requested is available.
- 201—This means that a new address was successfully created through a CGI or posting form data.

213

○ 202—The client's request was accepted, although not yet acted upon.

○ 203—The accepted information in the Entity header is not from the original server, but from a third party.

○ 204—There is no content in the requested click. Let's say that you click on an image map section not attached to a page. This allows the server to just sit there waiting for another click rather than throwing an error.

○ 205—This allows the server to reset the content returned by a CGI.

○ 206—Only partial content is being returned for some reason.

300-399 Codes

SRCs note that the request was not performed; a redirection is occurring. These are usually silent.

○ 300—The requested address refers to more than one entity. Depending on how the server is configured, you get an error or a choice of which page you want.

○ 301—Page has been moved permanently, and the new URL is available. You should be sent there by the server.

○ 302—Page has been moved temporarily, and the new URL is available. Your user should be sent by the server.

○ 303—This is a "see other" SRC. Data is somewhere else, and the GET method is used to retrieve it.

○ 304—This is a "Not Modified" SRC. If the header in the request asks "If Modified Since," this will return how long it's been since the page was updated.

○ 305—This tells the server that the requested document must be accessed by using the proxy in the Location header (that is, ftp, http).

400-499 Codes

The request is incomplete for some reason.

○ 400—There is a syntax error in the request. It is denied.

○ 401—The header in your request did not contain the correct authorization codes. You don't get to see what you requested.

○ 402—Payment is required. Don't worry about this one. It's not in use yet.

○ 403—You are forbidden to see the document you requested. It can also mean that the server doesn't have the capability to show you what you want to see.

- 404—Document not found. The page you want is not on the server nor has it ever been on the server. Most likely you have misspelled the title or used an incorrect capitalization pattern in the URL.

- 405—The method you are using to access the file is not allowed.

- 406—The page you are requesting exists, but you cannot see it because your own system doesn't understand the format the page is configured for.

- 407—The request must be authorized before it can take place.

- 408—The request timed out. For some reason, the server took too much time processing your request. Net congestion is the most likely reason.

- 409—Conflict. Too many people wanted the same file at the same time. It glutted the server. Try again.

- 410—The page use to be there, but now it's gone.

- 411—Your request is missing a Content-Length header.

- 412—The page you requested has some sort of pre-condition set up. This means that if something is a certain way, you can have the page. If you get a 412, that condition was not met. Oops!

- 413—Too big. What you requested is just too big to process.

- 414—The URL you entered is too long. Really! It's too long.

- 415—The page is an unsupported media type, like a proprietary file made specifically for a certain program.

500-599 Codes

Errors have occurred within the server itself.

- 501—What you requested of the server cannot be done by the server. Stop doing that you!

- 502—Your server has received errors from the server you are trying to reach. This is better known as the "Bad Gateway" error.

- 503—The format or service you are requesting is temporarily unavailable.

- 504—The gateway is timed out. This is a lot like the 408 error except the timeout occurred specifically at the gateway of the server.

- 505—The HTTP protocol you are asking for is not supported.

Alternative Printing

The best tutorials come from either readers asking how they can get a specific effect or readers sending me a command and asking what in the world it does. It just goes to show that people do look at each other's source code.

The other day, I received a submission from a friend at Dynamic Drive who asked if I had seen a certain command in action. I had seen the tag he was discussing, but never paid much attention to it because it didn't really do anything that I thought was all that great. I took another look.

 You can find this tutorial online at http://www.htmlgoodies.com/beyond/altprint.html.

You should know up front that at the time of this writing, this command is only supported by Internet Explorer 4.0 and above. I don't know that it can quite be referred to as DHTML because the effect isn't that dynamic.

It seems that my friend attempted to print a page, and it didn't print. Something printed, but it wasn't the page. Somehow the author had set it up so that when my friend attempted to print, what was actually sent to the printer was something else.

Here's What's Happening

The page that printed was what's known as an alternative page. A command was set in the HEAD tags that stepped in and redirected the print command that you sent to the browser. Basically, the author set up a route that moved the browser away from the current page and on to another. Here's the code that did it:

```
<link rel=alternate media=print href="printversion.txt">
```

That's it. Here's what's happening:

- link denotes the relationship of something being a link. That "something" will be set soon.
- rel denotes the relationship of this link. What it will do is set up an alternative to the default. In this case, the default will be to print the page. We're going to stop that.
- media tells the links what media to deal with. At the moment, only "print" is supported. Other attributes include Braille, handheld, screen, projection, and TV, but none are up and running yet.
- href tells the command to use this address as the alternative.

So What Actually Happened?

I set up the command so that it would step in and redirect the browser's print function to print another page. In this case, you printed `"printversion.txt"`. That page said that you didn't have permission to print the page.

It's pretty tricky, eh? You actually did print something, but the effect was that you were denied the ability to print. Please note that you can print other formats. When John sent me the command, he had it set to print a Word document. As long as the user's computer has the capability to read the page, it can be printed. I just went with a text page because I know that all computers, no matter what their level of advancement, can print text.

Other Uses

Outside of giving the impression that I stopped your ability to print, I see this being very helpful with forms or charts or just about any other support document required for a site. For example, maybe you have a page that requires a user to fill out a form. You could use this tag to make it so that all one needed to do was click the Print button and the form prints out. If you have a chart in XLS format, you could do the same.

I would use an internal browser test JavaScript to test the person's browser when using the command. You could set up the internal test so that if the user is running IE4 or better, the text would be written so that it reads, "To get the form, simply click your Print button." If the browser is different, set the JavaScript to write a hypertext link so that the user can go to a page and print the form.

I wish this command were more widely available because I see a great many uses for it. In fact, I intend to set up just such a format in one of my online classes. It would be a great way to distribute homework to students.

Students just love that homework, let me tell you.

Make Your Own PDF Pages

To the reader: At the time I set this tutorial to print, all the following links and prices were good. Because this book is static, it is quite possible that many price changes, redirects, and modifications have occurred.

 You can find this tutorial, and all of its examples, online at `http://www.htmlgoodies.com/tutors/pdf.html`.

One of the questions I get a lot at HTML Goodies is how one goes about making an Adobe Acrobat PDF (Portable Document Format) document for downloading.

I think most everyone has the Adobe Acrobat PDF reader. If not, why not? It's free. Grab it at `http://www.adobe.com/products/acrobat/readermain.html`.

That's a free download from the Adobe site at `http://www.adobe.com/`.

The problem is that the free software doesn't allow you to make your own PDF files. To do that, you need to get the pay for version. I wrote this tutorial on December 12, 2000, and at that time the Adobe site was selling the full Acrobat version 5.0 for just about $250. You find that here: `http://www.adobe.com/store/products/acrobat.html`.

The Acrobat InProduction software was a little more pricey at around $500. You'll find it here: `http://www.adobe.com/products/inproduction/main.html`. There's a deal to buy both at the same time, and if you go searching around on the Web, you'll save a few bucks.

So, there you go; to make PDF files, head to the Adobe site, drop a few hundred, and get the software.

Of course, that's not the end of the tutorial. That would seem a little goofy, eh? I decided to kill an afternoon and take a stroll around the Web just to see if there were easier, nay, cheaper, methods of getting your own PDF files. I found a few that range from just a few bucks to fully free.

Adobe Cheap

Adobe employees know that people like me will tell you where to get PDF files created, so they have attempted to counteract these quests by offering a service that will create a PDF for you. It's called "Create Adobe PDF Online." At the time of this writing, you could get a free trial that makes a few files or pay around $10 a month or $100 a year to make as many PDF files as you'd like. Visit the page at `http://www.adobe.com/store/products/createpdf.html`. If you'd like to get the information in PDF, try `http://www.adobe.com/products/acrobat/pdfs/accessbooklet.pdf`.

It seems like a nice cheap method because you'd need to be using the site for a little more than two years before you'd actually spend as much money as the software itself would cost.

Basically, you upload a word processor file (many formats are supported) or point the system to a Web page URL and the system does the rest. You choose to either download the fully formed PDF or have it sent to you as an email attachment. That's a deal!

txt2PDF.cgi

There's a Perl script floating around that you can install on your system that will make PDF files in much the same method as the Adobe service. Here's the link to search on Yahoo!: `http://google.yahoo.com/bin/query?p=txt2PDF&hc=0&hs=0`.

The code is shareware and does have a price attached, but it is much lower than buying the Adobe software. I found version 4.0 available for around $85 at the time of this writing. You'll find that the costs drop for earlier versions.

If you'd like a free trial version of CGI, try `http://www.sanface.com/createpdf.html`. That is available from SanFace.com. It runs version 2.0 of txt2PDF.cgi, and it works. I've tried it. The file took until the next day to arrive in my mailbox, but it arrived just fine. You'll note that this is not a full-page version deal. You need to copy and paste in to the screen, so text-only pages go best here. (Thus, it has the name, txt2PDF. Get it?) If text is all you want to do, this is a winner.

Win2PDF

There's a nice piece of shareware out there ($35 at the time of this writing) that will make a PDF from a series of file formats. Again, I haven't tried it, but it certainly got some pretty good reviews.

If you'd like to do a search to try and find it, here's the Yahoo! search for the software: `http://google.yahoo.com/bin/query?p=Win2PDF&hc=0&hs=0`.

Ghostview and Ghostscript

Here's your fully free PDF deal. This page sponsored by the University of Arizona is offering the Ghostview and Ghostscript software as free downloads complete with instructions: `http://www.u.arizona.edu/~bintiyot/howtoPDF.html#gs`.

I should state here again that I have not downloaded and tried this method. Furthermore, I cannot take any responsibility for what might happen if you install the software. I am simply making this method known to you. I don't know why there would be a problem, but for legal purposes, you try this method at your own risk. OK? OK!

The format is fully outlined on the page, but here's the basic push. You need to install a printer on your system that will save files as postscript. The page suggests the HP PaintJet XL300 Postscript . Yes, I know you don't own that printer. You don't need to. The author suggests that the printer might already be in your operating system software, so you won't even need any new software. What a great and wondrous world we live in.

After you have that pup installed, you will save the document you want to turn to PDF to that printer, except you will save it to file. You'll want to assure that the file saves with the extension .ps. It sometimes saves as .prn. You don't want that. Force the computer's hand and save as .ps.

Now it's super easy. Open your file system and click on the file. The PostScript panel will pop up. Choose the Ghostscript control panel and save the file as a PDF. The author has offered a few examples of documents he's saved through the system. I looked. They're pretty good.

Hopefully, you can find and use one of these pieces of software. I'm quite interested in whether any of you get the Ghost software to run. I haven't tried a lot of this software because I have access to the full version at my university. A short walk at lunch, and I'm done. Plus, I like the people who work in the faculty computer lab.

After you have the PDF file, getting it to display is just as easy as making a hypertext link right to the PDF file. The browser will do the rest. Just make sure that you upload the PDF file. That mistake is so common. When one of my images or files throws an error, I always check to make sure that I uploaded the item. More times than not, I didn't.

Oh well, recognize the same mistake...every time you make it.

OnError **Event Handler**

If you've ever been surfing and run in to Web pages that threw JavaScript errors, you know what a pain they can be. If you use a lot of JavaScript on your pages, you know that errors are just part of the game. No matter how careful you are, sometimes your pages throw errors.

It is my opinion that a user would much rather not see an error. That's why I like this simple little script so much.

JavaScript 1.1 allowed a new event handler named onerror. I've also seen it written onError and OnERROR. All three worked on my machines.

This Event Handler allows you to have something happen when the page throws an error. The way I've seen it used online is to tell the user what line the error came from. I guess that would be good for the developer, but I'm more concerned about the users. I have taken the onerror Event Handler and put it into a script that will redirect the user to a different page as soon as an error is thrown.

Because of the nature of the command, the user might never even know that an error has occurred. There won't be an error box. There won't be the nasty little yellow triangle in the status bar. There won't be anything...except a new page.

Now, it's up to you how you'd like to use this. I would suggest having a non-JavaScript form on the page. That means a little more work, but it will help to keep a JavaScript heavy site error free.

Without any more talking...here's the script:

```
<SCRIPT LANGUAGE="JavaScript1.1">
<!--
onerror = redirect;
function redirect()
{
parent.location='errorfreepage.html'
}
-->
</SCRIPT>
```

There's not much to it, eh? I do want to point out a few things though.

First, the SCRIPT flag does specifically denote JavaScript 1.1. The onerror Event Handler is set up to run a function titled redirect. When an error occurs, the function triggers and the page is changed through the "parent.location" hierarchy line.

It's easy. Here's the script in action. Click on the following URL. It will take you to a page titled, "jserrorpage.html". There is a JavaScript error on that page. When the error hits, the page should change to something I titled "errorfreepage".

Give it a shot. You'll find a working example at http://www.htmlgoodies.com/beyond/jserrorpage.html.

Put the script high on your page so that it is in RAM before any JavaScript errors can occur. That's the easy part. What you need to do now is figure out where you will send the people who arrive at a page that throws an error.

Flash Plug-in Test Page

You can use JavaScript to check for specific plug-ins. In this specific case, we're dealing with a Flash plug-in, and it's about time. I'm getting tired of all of the pages that ask whether I have Flash. Stop asking me. Test for me and then send me to a page that's optimized for my system. You're the Webmaster! Help me! Help me enjoy your page!!

Okay, then. My blood pressure is lowering.

There, that's better.

 You can find this tutorial, and all of its examples, online at http://www.htmlgoodies.com/beyond/flashtest.html.

 You can download just the examples at http://www.htmlgoodies.com/wpg/.

Lately, I have been seeing two methods of setting an immediate check for a Flash plug-in. One is done through Flash itself. Because I am nowhere near a Flash expert, I'll send you to the Macromedia site if you'd like to see that method. Here's a link to the page: http://www.macromedia.com/support/flash/ts/documents/scriptfree_detection.htm.

The problem with the methods noted previously, a firewall page and the Macromedia Flash format, is that both stop me at the front door of a site. I have to either make a choice or wait. My research, and just about every study I've read, suggests that the users do not want to be stopped. They would rather the choice be made for them.

Just as you can set a JavaScript to test for browser type, version, screen sizes, and internal parameters, you can also use JavaScript to test for plug-ins.

Let's do the Flash plug-in, shall we?

The Code

Although I enjoy writing most of the JavaScripts distributed on this site, I didn't write this one. In fact, I don't know who did. I found the script by doing a Google search on the words "Detect Flash Plugin." It seems like a stock script because I found it on numerous sites covering several different topics. It was used on at least 20 different sites that I found. At no time did I ever find a copyright or author name. That leads me to believe it's a distributed script.

Plus, one must enforce copyright or lose it. I'm going to offer it here mainly because it's the best script I've seen to this point in that it is easy to understand, gets the job done efficiently, and works like other browser detect scripts.

You'll take the following code and paste it in to a document. Nothing else should be placed in to the document you're making. Please note the BODY flag at the end. That's really important. It's what triggers the script and offers the two possible page destinations.

Here's the code—it's a full page from HTML to end HTML:

```
<HTML>
<HEAD>
<SCRIPT LANGUAGE="JavaScript">
<!--
function MM_checkPlugin(plgIn, theURL, altURL, autoGo)
{
//v3.0
var ok=false;
document.MM_returnValue = false;
with (navigator)
```

```
if (appName.indexOf('Microsoft')==-1)
ok=(plugins && plugins[plgIn]);
else if (appVersion.indexOf('3.1')==-1)
{
//not Netscape or Win3.1
if (plgIn.indexOf("Flash")!=-1 && window.MM_flash!=null)
ok=window.MM_flash;
else if (plgIn.indexOf("Director")!=-1 && window.MM_dir!=null)
ok=window.MM_dir;
else ok=autoGo;
}
if (!ok) theURL=altURL;
if (theURL) window.location=theURL;
}
//-->
</SCRIPT>
<META HTTP-EQUIV="refresh" CONTENT="8;
URL=NON-FLASHPAGE.html">
</HEAD>
<!-- Get what is below all onto one line -->
<!-- Get what is below all onto one line -->
<BODY BGCOLOR="#FFFFFF" onLoad="MM_checkPlugin('Shockwave Flash',
➥'FLASHPAGE.html','NON-FLASHPAGE.html',true);
➥return document.MM_returnValue">
<!-- Get what is above all onto one line -->
<!-- Get what is above all onto one line -->
</BODY>
</HTML>
```

Altering the Code

Basically, you'll need to make one change to the META command just above the /HEAD flag and two changes in the BODY flag. See where I have the code:

```
"'FLASHPAGE.html','NON-FLASHPAGE.html'"
```

Put in the address of the page that contains the Flash and then the address of the page that does not have the Flash where it suggests. Also, put the URL of the non-Flash page in the META flag. That's it.

There are a couple of downfalls to the script in that Flash cannot be detected in Netscape 2 or Explorer 3 and 4 on Mac and Konqueror. That's why I stuck that META command in there. I placed it after the JavaScript code and set it to eight seconds. That way if the script

223

fails to work because of the version bug, the page will change for the user. I would set that META link to the non-Flash page just to be sure.

There you go. Enjoy it. It's a nice little script to help out your Flash and non-Flash users.

XHTML

To the reader: I thought I'd leave you with a short glimpse into the possible future. XHTML, some say, is the way it's all going. Others disagree. I haven't quite made up my mind yet. Well, yes I have. I'm just not going to tell you my decision here.

 You can find this tutorial, and all of its examples, online at *http://www.htmlgoodies.com/ tutors/xhtml.html.*

Not too long ago, the World Wide Web Consortium (W3C) recommended HTML version 4.0 (and now version 4.01). I put up a tutorial on all the new HTML 4.0 commands, and then set about creating in-depth tutorials for each command.

It was only a matter of time before someone wrote to me and asked when HTML 5.0 would be coming out. I have your answers:

It never will.

It already has.

On January 26, 2000, the W3C released specifications defining what they termed XHTML 1.0 (Extensible Hypertext Markup Language). I have also seen it written as xHTML, Xhtml, and XML/HTML.

Now, depending on which articles you read, (I've read way too many at this point), XHTML is either HTML 5.0, or HTML versions breathed their last with 4.0 and there will never be a 5.0 because XHTML is the direction markup languages are taking now.

Confused? Let's beat through it.

Right now there are two languages vying to be number one on the Web. The first is good old HTML, and the second is Extensible Markup Language (XML). Which is better really depends on whom you talk to and what they want to do with the pages they create.

HTML is well within the grasp of the Weekend Silicon Warrior and creates decent text and image pages. It is, by far, the most-used language on the Web.

XML is more dynamic and allows for more specific database interaction than was ever possible before. An example would be searching for "dog" in Yahoo!. You get everything that has "dog," as well as all related, larger words such as "dogma." Well, XML can change all that. Your searches and requests can be specific. Results will be specific.

Another big plus on the XML side is the ability for you to create custom XML tags. If you want a tag named "zork" that allows you to turn text green and change the font size to 24 point, you can create it.

What Is This XHTML?

Once again, some say it's HTML with XML qualities. Others, like me, say it's XML with HTML written into the Document Type Definition (DTD).

Here's the scoop as I understand it. XML has become the chosen language for the Web's future. At least, that's the feeling I get from reading the pages on the W3C Web site. Obviously, you cannot simply eliminate HTML, so the W3C did what, I think, was a pretty smart thing. They combined them. I just don't know that I'm overly thrilled with the way they combined them.

Document Type Definition: DTD

Inside your browser, there's a DTD. It's different from browser to browser depending on which version you're using. Internet Explorer 4.0 understands some HTML 4.0 level commands and Internet Explorer 3.0 doesn't because those commands were written in to the 4.0 browser's DTD.

The new XHTML 1.0 DTD, looks like this:

```
http://www.w3.org/TR/xhtml1/DTD/xhtml1-strict.dtd
```

It is basically the XML DTD with the HTML 4.0 DTD put inside it. Users must follow the majority of XML rules because HTML is under XML's umbrella rather than being the other way around.

Why?

The W3C suggests that HTML should be "an application of XML." The purpose is to tighten HTML's programming standards to make them compliant with XML.

You might not like that, but there's some sense to it. XML is very specific. One thing means one thing, period. HTML isn't so specific. For example:

Tags can be in caps or not.

`Textarea` boxes require end tags, yet text boxes do not.

Tags can end in any order regardless of how they were placed.

I'm sure that you can come up with some more examples, but these are the three that I point out to students.

By placing the HTML 4.0 DTD under the XML DTD, the language has no choice but to follow the same strict rules that XML does. Some will love that, but others won't.

The Rules

At the moment, the best one can hope to do is to write XHTML documents that are compatible with current browsers. I'll run down a few of the rules for writing in XHTML. If you've already read my XML tutorial, many of them will be familiar to you.

1. *You will use the XML and XHTML declaration statements to start every XHTML page.*

```
<?xml version="1.0" encoding="UTF-8"?>
<!DOCTYPE html PUBLIC "-//W3C//DTD XHTML 1.0 Strict//EN"
"DTD/xhtml1-strict.dtd">
```

The commands will alert the browser displaying the page that XHTML is the language to render.

2. *The HEAD and BODY tags are now mandatory.*

3. *Every tag must be closed.*

In HTML, you could get away with simply putting a <P> between paragraphs, and the browser would render it just fine. If you only had one table on a page, you didn't need the end TD and end TR tags. Under the XHTML DTD, that's no longer true. All tags that require end tags get end tags.

4. *Empty tags get a terminating slash.*

An empty tag is a tag that doesn't require an end tag. Examples include <BR> and <HR>.

Under the XHTML DTD, empty tags will now carry a space following the tag text and then a terminating slash, like so:

```
<BR> is now <br />.
<HR> is now <hr />.<
<IMG SRC="--"> is now <img src="--" />.
```

You might have noticed here that I wrote HEAD, body, br, hr, and img in lowercase in the XHTML examples. That's because…

226

5. *All tags must be lowercase.*

This does not apply to attributes, only tags. For example, both of these formats are acceptable under the XHTML DTD:

```
<font color="#ffffcc">
<font color="#FFFFCC">
```

You might have noticed that I have quotes around all the attributes. That's because...

6. *Attribute quotes are now mandatory.*

7. *Tags may not nest.*

In HTML, this is an acceptable format. It will render

```
<B><I>Text</B></I>
```

Now the tags must follow a logical begin and end pattern. They must end at the same level as they are started. This is the proper XHTML method of writing the preceding code:

```
<b><i>Text</i></b>
```

Once again, note the lowercase tags.

8. *Attribute values must be denoted.*

Most attributes are done this way (for example, FONT FACE="arial"). Notice that "arial" follows the attribute "FACE=".

The attribute and equal signs, in some cases, have been eliminated in HTML. For example:

```
<INPUT TYPE="radio" checked>
```

The word checked is a minimized attribute. Under XHTML, that won't work. You must denote every attribute. Here's the correct method of writing the preceding code under the XHTML DTD:

```
<input type="radio" checked="checked">
```

These don't come up too often. Here are a few examples in HTML format:

```
<INPUT TYPE="radio" checked>
<INPUT TYPE="checkbox" checked>
<OPTION selected>
<DL compact>
<UL compact>
```

227

In each case, you'll need to set the minimized attribute to one that is denoted. The easy way to remember it is that it always denotes itself: `checked="checked"` and `selected="selected"`.

9. *The* `<pre>` *tag cannot contain:* `img`, `object`, `big`, `small`, `sub`, *or* `sup`.

10. *You may not have any forms inside of other forms.*

11. *If your code contains an* &, *it must be written as* `&amp`.

12. *Any use of CSS should use all lowercase lettering.*

13. *Any use of JavaScript should be done through external JavaScripting.*

Okay, this is not always true. You can set up a JavaScript within an XHTML DTD page. Here's a look at the format:

```
<script language="JavaScript type=text/javascript">
<![CDATA[
document.write("Hi there");
]]>
</script>
```

I think you'll agree; my previous statement, although not totally true, will save you multiple HEADaches.

14. `<!--Comments are no longer used-->`

If you want to write a comment in an XHTML document, you write it as

```
<[CDATA[comment goes in here]]>
```

15. *JavaScripts are no longer commented out.*

That will throw big errors in some browsers.

XHTML: Good or Bad?

I guess, once again, that depends on whom you talk to. The W3C says the two main selling points are *extensibility* and *portability*. I'll add *standardization* to that.

- Extensibility—XHTML is extendable. You can create your own tags and add onto them.

- Portability—Those new tags are done in such a way that all can understand it. (See the tutorial.)

- Standardization—Now we have a true template for what is and is not acceptable coding. Everyone must follow that template.

On the other side of the coin, I see a couple of problems.

- XHTML is not as easy to just play around with on the weekend as HTML. HTML is a sort of computer tinker toy that everyone can use. People might lose interest being held to such a rigid set of rules. But you can still write your HTML document just as you always did. The XHTML DTD contains HTML. You just need to use an HTML declaration statement at the top of the document.

- XHTML, and XML for that matter, go directly against the rules the W3C laid down for Web content and authoring tools accessible to disabled users.

I guess it's that first concern that worries me the most. I just don't want HTML to become a ghost hiding behind a language that the average Joe can't pick up. I wouldn't want those who run the coding show to "take back" programming on the Web by making it too difficult. I just hate the thought of that.

An Example

I took this example straight from the W3C's XHTML 1.0 page:

```
<?xml version="1.0" encoding="UTF-8"?>
<!DOCTYPE html
PUBLIC "-//W3C//DTD XHTML 1.0 Strict//EN"
"DTD/xhtml1-strict.dtd">
<html xmlns="http://www.w3.org/1999/xhtml" xml:lang="en" lang="en">
<HEAD>
<title>Virtual Library</title>
</HEAD>
<body>
<p>Moved to <a href="http://vlib.org/">vlib.org</a>.</p>
</body>
</html>
```

As you can see, the coding is very strict and maybe a little complicated for the HTML enthusiast. The language is available right now if you want to try it out. I would suggest using an Internet Explorer 5.0 level browser. Follow the rules laid out in this tutorial and the XML custom tags tutorial.

Write slowly and deliberately. HTML was forgiving. XHTML is not. You might want to read a bit more and look at some XHTML source codes by visiting some Yahoo! XHTML pages at `http://search.yahoo.com/bin/search?p=xhtml`.

Many of the pages offering help are actually written in XHTML.

After you're finished writing, use the W3C Validator Service to check your work: `http://validator.w3.org/`.

I don't see HTML ever going the way of the dinosaur, but I do expect to see it becoming more and more rigid under the XML umbrella. It's only a matter of time before all major search engines and server systems choose XML for database programming. HTML will need to start working under their choices.

Thanks to XHTML, you'll be able to continue writing in the HTML you've come to know and love. You just might need to clean it up a bit.

My guess is that XHTML 2.0 will specifically clean up HTML tags and their usage.

Epilogue

Well, how was it?

I hope you enjoyed the book. I hope you found something you could use. Better yet, I hope something within the book has sparked you to go further.

I've had a metal picture of most readers beating through this book, closing the back cover, laying it on top of the pile and asking, "What's next?"

Well, what's next is up to you. If you've gotten through this book and truly understand what's inside, you probably are fairly well versed in HTML and not too bad in JavaScript.

OK, what's next?

What's next can be answered by looking to the Web you're writing for. The best hint I can give to help you pick your next direction is to look at the extensions on the Web. I believe those are the best indicators of what's to come.

Are you seeing a lot of ASP extensions? How about that? Maybe that's your next direction. How about XML? Look not only at the extensions of the pages but also at the elements contained within the pages. Flash, streaming video and audio of every kind, images, Perl, or any number of server programming formats are all fodder for new directions.

Take my word for it: Those who work the Web will continue to come up with new formats and new languages or advance those that are already in use so often that you could pick any path and become consumed just the same way as Web design first consumed you.

You're at the advanced level in this area. Maybe it's time to start at the primer level of a new area.

I'm actually taking the time to read up on the laws associated with the Web.

It's a new area...

Index

How can we make this index more useful? Email us at indexes@quepublishing.com.

237

P-Q

page breaks, printing Web pages, 109-110
page redirection, 89-91
    scripts, 91-92
pages. *See also* Web pages
    alternative, 216-217
    home, Internet Explorer, 99
    PDF, creating, 217-218
    printing, 105-107
        colors, 108
        formats, 107-108
        images, 109
        page breaks, 109-110
        typography, 108
    Web, errors, 220-221
plug-ins, 221-224
    printing, 105-107
    refreshing, 196-197
    reloading, 196-198
parameters, wave filters (Internet Explorer), 65-66
passwords, JavaScript, 167
    arrays, 170-173
    code, 167-170, 172-173
    encrypted through arrays, 167
    hidden script, 167
PDF (Portable Document Format), 217
    files
        Ghostscript software, 219-220
        Ghostview software, 219-220
        Perl, 218
        txt2PDF.cgi, 219
        Win2PDF, 219
    pages, creating, 217-218
    Perl, PDF files, 218
        txt2PDF.cgi, 219

Perl SSIs, 10
    ASP, 14
    file returns, 20
    include command, 11
        arguments, 12
        file argument, 12
        files, 13-14
        virtual argument, 13
    includes, 18
        codes, 19-20
        date and time, 18-20
        echo command, 18, 21
        flastmod command, 21
        fsize command, 22
        timefmt argument, 19
    running, 10-11
    servers, 10
PFR (Portable Font Resource), 81
placing
    cookies, 184
    multiple, cookies, 184-185
plug-ins (Flash), 221-224
point variable, 145
pop-under windows, 120-122
Portable Document Format. *See* PDF
Portable Font Resource (PFR), 81
Pragma statement, 210-211
preloading images, 36
printing
    alternative, 216-217
        usage, 217
    pages, 105-107
        colors, 108
        formats, 107-108
        images, 109
        page breaks, 109-110
        typography, 108

prompts, JavaScript escape characters, 22-23
properties, HTA files, 199-201
protecting JavaScript passwords, 167
    arrays, 170-173
    code, 167-170, 172-173
    encrypted through arrays, 167
    hidden script, 167
putCookie() function, 180

R

rectangle, selection (Internet Explorer), 99-101
redirection, pages, 89-92
resizeTo() function, 105
resizing Browser window, 102-105
responses, servers, 212
    404 Error, 212-213
results
    cookie counters, 185
    copying to clipboard, 155-156
    maximizing screens, 195-196
    minimizing screens, 195-196
    setting cookies, 182
retrieving cookies, 182-184
revealTrans() filter, 54
    removing images, 54-55
    transition numbers, 55-56
        reversing effects, 56-58
right clicks (mouse), 190-191
rounded corners, tables, 111-112
    corner images, 113

Hey, you've got enough worries.

Don't let IT training be one of them.

Get on the fast track to IT training at InformIT,
your total Information Technology training network.

 | **www.informit.com** |

■ Hundreds of timely articles on dozens of topics ■ Discounts on IT books from all our publishing partners, including Que Publishing ■ Free, unabridged books from the InformIT Free Library ■ "Expert Q&A"—our live, online chat with IT experts ■ Faster, easier certification and training from our Web- or classroom-based training programs ■ Current IT news ■ Software downloads ■ Career-enhancing resources

Web Developer Resources

www.internet.com/webdev

www.gif.com

jobs.webdeveloper.com

www.javaboutique.com

www.justsmil.com

www.webdevelopersjournal.com

www.flashplanet.com

www.scriptsearch.com

www.wdvl.com

www.javascript.com

www.streamingmediaworld.com

www.webdeveloper.com

www.javascriptsource.com

webdesign.thelist.com

www.webreference.com

www.xml101.com

internet.com's Web Developer Channel is the Web's leading gathering place for the developer community. Member sites feature information resources that help developers do their jobs better, product reviews of key developer products and collections of scripts and applets to add to sites to enhance their performance. Reach this community of users – individuals who greatly influence the purchase of products and services – when they're proactively seeking professional information and technology solutions.

The Internet & IT Network